1,001
LOGICAL LAWS,
ACCURATE AXIOMS,
PROFOUND PRINCIPLES,
TRUSTY TRUISMS,
HOMEY HOMILIES,
COLORFUL COROLLARIES,
QUOTABLE QUOTES,
AND RAMBUNCTIOUS RUMINATIONS
FOR ALL WALKS OF LIFE...

"HILARIOUSLY PROFOUND!"
—*Detroit Free Press*

1,001

Logical Laws,
Accurate Axioms,
Profound Principles,
Trusty Truisms,
Homey Homilies,
Colorful Corollaries,
Quotable Quotes,
and
Rambunctious Ruminations
for all walks of life

Compiled by John Peers, President,
Logical Machine Corporation

Edited by Gordon Bennett

Illustrated by George Booth

FAWCETT COLUMBINE ● NEW YORK

1,001 LOGICAL LAWS

THIS BOOK CONTAINS THE COMPLETE TEXT OF THE ORIGINAL HARDCOVER EDITION.

Published by Fawcett Columbine Books, a unit of CBS Publications, the Consumer Publishing Division of CBS Inc., by arrangement with Doubleday and Company, Inc.

ISBN: 0-449-90014-2

Printed in the United States of America

First Fawcett Columbine printing: May 1980

10 9 8 7 6 5 4 3 2 1

Contents

Introduction

John Peers, our aphorism compiler, as president of Logical Machine Corporation was referred to as the Monty Python of the computer industry. Anyone who has met this especially enthusiastic and witty Englishman will agree that the description is apt. John Peers has some exceptionally notable ideas on computing, the computer industry, and promotion. The foremost of these ideas is stated in Peers's Law, which is: "The solution to a problem changes the nature of the problem." To make a long story short, Peers refers to the way in which many present-day computer solutions often create greater problems. To convey this point, he used his simple philosophy in a couple of advertisements in *The New Yorker* for his ADAM computer and asked readers to send in their favorite principle, axiom, homily, truism, quote, or rumination. The response was overwhelming; the result is this book.

George Booth, our aphorism illustrator, is called by some the funniest cartoonist in America. Since 1970 his drawings in *The New Yorker* have been those of one who chuckles at life, which made him the obvious choice to illustrate our book. The simplicity of his drawings demonstrates a thorough understanding of what makes plain dogs, plain cats, and plain people tick (not necessarily in that order). George was born in 1926 in Cainsville, a town of seven hundred people in north-central Missouri. An ex-marine, he served in World War II and the Korean "police action"; it was during the later stint that he became a cartoonist for the *Leatherneck* magazine. He attended George Washington University, Chicago Academy of Fine Arts, New York School of Visual Arts, and Adelphi University. He is at present a contract cartoonist for *The New*

Yorker and free-lance cartoonist. He has illustrated for such books as: *Think Good Thoughts About a Pussycat, Dogs,* and *Rehearsal's Off!*

Webster says an aphorism is "a short sentence stating a general truth or practical observation." This being the case, as our book points up, there's an awful lot of undiscovered philosophers in this world. The published submissions are from all walks of life and for all walks of life. They're hundreds of conclusions with a whimsical touch, a poignant principle, a succinct slant, and all with an obvious understanding of what it's all about. Oh, there are a few comments thrown in from such notables as Shaw, Twain, Teller, and Murphy (whoever he is), but most are from just plain people, who for a few fleeting moments have been just as keen observers of the action on life's stage as those who, so far, have received all the credit.

This book, as a compilation of sage statements, is full of belly laughs, and that's as it should be. But students of the "ologies" will find an earthy basicness throughout that will stimulate their comprehension of everyday society.

On top of all that, it will make each and everyone who reads it a brilliant conversationalist.

1,001
LOGICAL LAWS,
ACCURATE AXIOMS,
PROFOUND PRINCIPLES,
TRUSTY TRUISMS,
HOMEY HOMILIES,
COLORFUL COROLLARIES,
QUOTABLE QUOTES,
AND RAMBUNCTIOUS RUMINATIONS
FOR ALL WALKS OF LIFE...

Terman's Law:
>   There is no direct relationship between the quality of an educational program and its cost.

Campbell's Traveling-with-the-Kids Law:
>   It's better to go when you have to go—than to go and find you've already gone.

Hendrickson's Law:
>   If a problem causes many meetings, the meetings eventually become more important than the problem.

The George Washington Cherry Tree Theory of Truth and Consequences:
>   You can get away with anything as long as you tell someone about it.

Mark Twain's Observation:
>   Adam was but human—this explains it all. He did not want the apple for the apple's sake, he wanted it because it was forbidden.

Saul Lavisky's Observation:
>   Education is what you get from reading the small print. Experience is what you get from not reading it.

Rahilly's Law of Academic Administration:
>Remember that not all the faculty have all their faculties.

Haap's Rule:
>Don't ever let an alligator mouth overload a hummingbird rear end.

Papa Rich's Conclusion:
>Whatever a parent does is wrong.

Kavanaugh's Maxim:
>Necessity never made a good bargain.

Zaenglein's Postulate:
>Kids used to ask you where they came from—now they tell you where to go.

Rodney's Rule:
>Never let your studies interfere with your education.

McFadden's Observation:
>The trouble with experience as a teacher is that the test comes first and the lesson afterward.

The First Afghan Law of Education:
>No amount of poor schooling can spoil a good student.

Sanders' Rumination:
>Life is a game, the object of which is to discover the object of the game.

Cornuelle's Law:
>Authority tends to assign jobs to those least able to do them.

Clint's Cure-All:
>When in danger or in doubt, run in circles, scream and shout!

Mullins' Observation:
>Indecision is the key to flexibility.

Father Brennan's Famous Footnote:
>Children should be heard, not obscene.

Baird's Rumination:
>The brilliant person who invented peanut butter can't be all that great.

Napier's Cogent Comment:
>Old people know more about being young than young people about being old.

Hecker's Law:
>If you do your lessons every day, you never have to worry about a test.

Boxer's Law:
>A person who minces his words usually chokes on them.

Mrs. Bowman's Law of Sibling Rivalry:
>The child who cuts the piece of candy in half doesn't get first choice of the two pieces.

Engle's Law:
>Don't ever stand up to be counted or someone will take your seat.

Preston's Postulate:

> He who trains his tongue to quote the learned sages will be known far and wide as a smart-ass.

Jimenez's Maxim:

> If they give you ruled paper, write the other way.

An Educational Guess:

> The founder of the school of hard knocks bruised easily.

Spence's Observation:

> One doesn't have to be handicapped to get a good education, but it certainly helps.

Shultz's Sage Thought:

> If you don't have a memory like an elephant, leave tracks like one.

Parker's Rule of Parliamentary Procedure:

> A motion to adjourn is always in order,

Grandma Soderquist's Observation:

> Remember on your walk through life, the grass made greener on the other side of the fence is caused by "pasture pies."

Sousa's Principle of Lecture:

> If you can't baffle them with brilliance, befuddle them with bullshit.

Talamantez's Gripe:

> You don't discover life is more than a bowl of cherries till after you've eaten them.

Groya's Law:
> What we learn after we know it all, is what counts.

Dr. Levitan's Rule:
> If it smells bad and is sticky, it will eventually find its way onto your children or your shoes.

Furst's Academic Axiom:
> He who controls the purse strings controls the educational policy.

Utvich's Observation:
> Education is the process of moving from cocksure ignorance to thoughtful uncertainty.

B. V. Roy's Conclusion:
> Teaching is the fine art of imparting knowledge without possessing it.

Bergman's Bromide:
> Today's life-style is such that no matter how much money you make, you'll still eat hamburger (in some form) four times a week.

Goldstein's Truism:
> Success means only doing what you do well, letting someone else do the rest.

Oscar Mayer's Creed:
> No matter how many hot dogs you consume at home, they always taste better at the ball park.

Polis' Attorney's Law:
>   Any law enacted with more than fifty words contains at least one loophole.

Metzger's Maxim:
>   A "government subsidy" is getting just some of your own money back.

Anthony's Observations:
>   (1)   Freedom requires every man beware those that share his views.
>   (2)   Exceptions rule.
>   (3)   People, judging an entirely new matter, will be:
>   one third in favor
>   one third opposed, and
>   one third undecided.
>   (4)   President, beware a mood of nostalgia that occurs during your Administration.
>   (5)   Join the Republican party if you cannot abide Democrats. You will probably loathe Republicans just as much, but there are fewer of them.
>   (6)   The English language has so few cuss words that, much like the flag, they should not be displayed day after day, but kept inside, lovingly rolled up and stored away, to bring forth proudly, unfaded, and effective upon special occasions.

Adam's Admonition:
>   Those who like sausage or political policy should not watch it being made.

Abraham Lincoln's Rumination:
>   Tell the truth and you won't have so much to remember.

Mo Udall's First Law of Politics:
>   If you can't find something everyone agrees on, it's wrong.

Mo Udall's Second Law of Politics:
>   It's hard to convince people of the first.

Murray's Law:
>   If written correctly, legalese is perfectly incomprehensible.

The "What Am I Doing Here?" Rule:
>   It's better to leave the room than try to make an explanation when something doesn't work.

Grandma Soderquist's Rule for Political Speeches:
>   Don't ever make a speech with more than one thousand words. The speech should contain and repeat certain key words like: "people," 81 times; "our country," 26 times; "liberty," 17 times; "the poor," 33 times; "I promise you," 77 times; and call all opponents "incompetent" as many times as you can say it.

Hodges' Observation:
>   The problem with government is that it scratches where there ain't no itch.

Vietnam Corollary:
>   If you expected it to be easy, you should have become a politician.

Van Roy's Postulates:

   (1) Government always plays both ends against the tax-payer.

   (2) Inflation is a stab in the buck.

The Abilene Paradox:

   People in groups tend to agree on courses of action which, as individuals, they know are stupid.

Boyle's Observation:

   A welfare state is one that assumes responsibility for the health, happiness, and general well-being of all its citizens except the taxpayers.

Observation by a Mad Author:

   If you tell the truth once, they will never believe you again, no matter how much you lie.

Andrew's Truism:

   Honesty is almost always the best policy.

Johnson's First Law of Politics:

   As soon as you're elected, get that "Honorable" in front of your name.

George Bernard Shaw's Observation:

   Those who can—do. Those who cannot—teach.

H. L. Mencken's Corollary:

   Those who can't teach—administrate. Those who can't administrate—run for office.

Archimedes' Principle of Politics:

   A light-weight congressman can often be buoyed up by a force equal to the weight of the pork in his barrel.

The Politician's Rule:
> In politics you can often be wrong, but never in doubt.

Kling's Contrast:
> Statesmen tell you what is true even though it may be unpopular. Politicians tell you what is popular even though it may be untrue.

Dr. Nordstrom's First Rule of Debate:
> It is difficult to win an argument when your opponent is unencumbered with a knowledge of the facts.

Hawkinson's Law:
> Every clarification breeds new questions.

Kamin's Law:
> Politicians will always inflate when given the opportunity.

Calvin Coolidge's Comment:
> We cannot do everything at once, but we can do something at once.

Kamin's Law of Politics:
> When attempting to predict and forecast microeconomic moves or economic legislation by a politician, never be misled by what he says; instead watch what he does.

H. L. Mencken's Observation:
> The main trouble with democracy is that the people eventually realize that they can vote themselves the treasury; then you have anarchy.

Parker's Law of Political Statements:
> The truth of a proposition has nothing to do with its credibility and vice versa.

Jacquin's Postulate on Democratic Governments:

> No man's life, liberty, or property are safe while the legislature is in session.

Expression from a Politician Who Didn't Wish to be Quoted:

> Long ago we forgot that what was best for most of the people was best for all the people.

Hoffman's Rule:

> Smile—it makes people wonder what you're thinking.

Ferdinand Lundberg's Law:

> There is such thing as a "cheap politician."

Pate's Prattle:

> Bureaucrats are the meat loaf of humanity.

Nowlan's Deduction:

> Following the path of least resistance is what makes men and rivers crooked.

White's Chappaquiddick Theorem:

> The sooner and in more detail you announce bad news, the better.

Sorenson's Law:

> If you want to make it in politics, go to church regularly.

Doelger's Findings:

> Politician's political issues are true enough—only their facts have been made up.

Taft's Law:

> If "pro" is the opposite of "con," then "Progress" is the opposite of "Congress."

Imhoff's Law:

> The organization of any bureaucracy is very much like a septic tank—the really big chunks always rise to the top.

The First Law of an Officeholder:
Get re-elected.

Henry's Political Pragmatism:
To run for a political office, all it takes is a few bucks, a pretty face, a glib tongue, a church membership, a large family, and absolutely no sense of economics.

Clarke's Law of Revolutionary Ideas:
Every revolutionary idea—in science, politics, art, or whatever—evokes three stages of reaction in a hearer:
(1) It is completely impossible—don't waste my time.
(2) It is possible, but it is not worth doing.
(3) I said it was a good idea all along.

Gordon's Law for Politicians:
When you get a chance to get any podium—don't rush it, keep smiling, shake as many hands as possible, yell "John and Mary" (as many common names as possible), and upon arriving nod several times, grab both sides of the podium, lean forward slowly, look stern, stare at the back of the hall for several moments, etc. The idea is to open your mouth as little as possible.

Justice Douglas' Observation:
The right to be left alone is indeed the beginning of all freedom.

Hodghead's Cynicism:
A husband (or wife) is a person who sticks with you through troubles you wouldn't have had if you hadn't married him (or her) in the first place.

Hildebrant's Rule:
True wealth is not so much having talent, industry, and a bit of luck, as it is having lots of money.

Ellis' Eloquence:

    (1)   To find a policeman in a hurry, double-park.

    (2)   Start your own lay-a-way plan . . . smoke.

    (3)   If God thought that nudity was O.K., we would have been born naked.

Peers's Possibility:

    Too many books you can tell by their cover.

Alfred E. Smith's Rule:

    No matter how thin you slice it, it's still baloney.

Aphorisms for Politicians from the *Congressional Record:*

    (1)   You have to know what's biting you before you reach for a remedy.

    (2)   Always look for the calculations that go with the calculated risks.

    (3)   Try to find out who's doing the work, not who's writing about it, controlling it, or summarizing it.

    (4)   Watch out for formal briefings. They often produce an avalanche (definition: a high-level snow job of massive and overwhelming proportions).

    (5)   The difficulty of the co-ordination task often blinds one to the fact that a fully co-ordinated piece of paper is not supposed to be either the major or the final product of the organization, but it often turns out that way.

    (6)   Most organizations can't hold more than one idea at a time . . . thus complementary ideas are always regarded as competitive. Further, like a consistent pendulum, an organization can jump from one extreme to another, without ever going through the middle.

Lyndon's Observation:

    If the first person who answers the phone cannot answer your question, it's a bureaucracy.

☞ Quotes for Those Buffs Who Like to Needlepoint Signs for Around the Home

Pulliam's Postulate:
> Never step in anything soft.

Dad's Law:
> The most valuable gift you can give your family is a good example.

Steven's Rule:
> One man's trash is another man's treasure.

Ornstein's Law:
> Nobody ever puts out a sign that says NICE DOG.

Stoddart's Wisdoms:
> (1) Beat your child once a day. If you don't know why, he does.
> (2) If you would avoid suspicion, do not stoop to lace your shoes in a melon patch.

Chuck's Conclusion:
> A small carafe of wine is illogical, immoral, and inadequate.

Professor Dillon Rule:
> A God we can understand is no God.

Nancy's Maxim:
    A poor excuse is better than no excuse at all.

Welch's Words:
    An honest answer can get you into a lot of trouble.

Fruit of the Loom Fruity Comment:
    Don't sell America shorts.

Ben Franklin's Wisdom:
    (1)   Success has ruined many a good man.
    (2)   If a man could have half his wishes, he would double his troubles.
    (3)   If passion drives you, let reason hold the reins.
    (4)   Anger is never without reason, but seldom with a good one.
    (5)   If every fool wore a crown, we would all be kings.
    (6)   Little strokes fell great oaks.

Mrs. Murphy's Law:
    The average woman talks 50 per cent more than her husband listens.

Hill's Corollary of Alimentation:
    If God had meant for us to consume peanut butter, He would have lined our mouths with Teflon.

Cannon's Cogent Comments:
    (1)   A major cause of divorce is a man's inability to start the outboard motor on the first ten tries.
    (2)   The cops are *always* around when you *don't* want them.

Hardyman's Truism:
    Random stomping seldom catches bugs.

Preston's Postulates:
    (1)   He who uses bad language is an ignorant shnuck.
    (2)   Love thy neighbor, but be sure her husband is away.
    (3)   Two can live as cheaply as one . . . for half as long.

Kelley's Observation:
    Father's day is just like Mother's day—except he gets a cheaper gift.

Cooper's Law of Affection:
    Home is where, if you have no place to go, they gotta take you in.

More Van Roy's Postulates:
    (1)   Swallow much but digest little.
    (2)   Never change diapers in midstream.
    (3)   When you go on a diet, the first thing you lose is your temper.

Radar's Fundamental Truth:
    The grass is brown on both sides of the fence.

Rosner's Rules:
    (1)   Where there's a will, there are five hundred relatives.
    (2)   It takes two to make a marriage—a girl and her mother.

Allen's Observation:
    There's no such thing as a "simple little job around the house."

The Backed-Up Bathroom Bromide:
    The spirit is willing—but the flush is weak.

The Gordian Maxim:
    If a string has one end, it has another.

The Junk Mail Law:
>   The mailman bringeth and the trashman taketh away.

Boob Tube Truism:
>   Turn the dial to see what's on another channel—you'll hit a commercial.

The Prodigal Son's Lament:
>   Home is where, when they feed you rutabagas, you have to eat them.

Norman's Household Hint:
>   Give me a home where the buffalo roam, and you've got a room full of buffalo chips.

Doelger's Law:
>   Always find out what the kids are doing and tell them to stop.

Renau's Rural Ramblings:
>   A hole in the bottom of a bird's nest usually means she enjoys laying eggs, but is not fond of children.

Jason's Law:
>   An unbreakable toy is good for breaking other toys.

Flynn's Rumination:
>   If I had my life to live over again, I'd make the same mistakes sooner.

☞ For the Medically Minded—Some Thoughts to Operate By

Tuttle's First Law of Pollution:
> You're never more than a few feet away from a product containing PCB.

Macaluso's Doctrine:
> You've never been as sick as just before you stop breathing.

Clifford's Proclamation:
> VD is nothing to clap about.

Gynecologist's Remark:
> I've had a busy day at the orifice.

Crosby's Deduction:
> Old doctors never die, they just lose their patients.

Dusinberre's Conclusion:
> I'm not in the practice of medicine for my health, because it ain't healthy.

Barach's Rule:
> An alcoholic is a person who drinks more than his own physician.

Shalit's Drugstore Observation:
These pills can't be habit-forming; I've been taking them for years.

Pollack's Prognosis:
Things only turn out well in the end if you visit a proctologist.

The Surgeon's Quandary:
Oops—I cut it off again and it's still too short.

Borland's Postulate:
All gall is divided into three parts: bladder, stones, and unmitigated.

Goldstein's Axiom:
The dentist never talks to his patients until the drill is in their mouths.

Knebel's Law:
It is now proved beyond doubt that smoking is one of leading causes of statistics.

The "What's Wrong With Me, Doctor?" Law:
Wait, we'll see what the computer says.

Loeb's Laws of Medicine:
(1) If what you're doing is working, keep doing it.
(2) If what you're doing is not working, stop doing it.
(3) If you don't know what to do, don't do anything.
(4) Above all, never let a surgeon get your patient.

Dr. Van Sickle's Theory:
Basically the function of the heart is to keep pumping.

Rumple's Rule:
> No hospital staff physician is totally worthless; he can always be used as a horrible example.

The Patient's Rule Concerning his Symptoms:
> It's not a matter of life or death—it's much more important than that.

Merskey's Rules:
> (1)   Do a silly test and you get a silly answer.
>
> (2)   In the hospital more deaths occur in bed than out of bed, so get the patient out of bed.
>
> (3)   Any drug can do anything.

Danowski's Laws:
> (1)   It takes two years to learn when to go into the abdomen and twenty years to learn when to stay out.
>
> (2)   A drug is that substance which when injected into rat will produce a scientific report.

Hart's Inverse-Care Law:
> The availability of good medical care tends to vary inversely with the need for it in the population.

Frisch's Law:
> It takes one woman nine months to have a baby, no matter how many men you put on the job.

Firestone's Negative Reformulation of Frisch's Law:
> You cannot have a baby in one month by getting nine women pregnant.

Dr. Cohen's First Rule of Clinical Medicine:
> What you don't take can't hurt you.

Launegayer's Observation:

Vampires are poor unfortunate souls suffering from iron deficiency anemia who have never heard of Geritol.

Schmidt's Law:

Never eat prunes when you're hungry.

Dr. Tobias' Conclusion:

The secret of good health is eating a raw onion a day. Trouble is, no one can keep it a secret.

Harvard's Law:

Under the most rigorously controlled conditions of pressure, temperature, volume, humidity, and other variables, the organism will do as it damn well pleases.

Swine Flu Shot Definition:

A cure for which there is no known disease.

Wendell's Observation:

No need to give up the race just because you joggle when you jog.

☞ AXIOMS FOR THE COMPUTER AGE, AND OTHERS

Gross's Postulate:

> Facts are not all equal. There are good facts and bad facts. Science consists of using good facts.

Utz's Laws of Computer Programming:

> (1)   Any given program, when running, is obsolete.
>
> (2)   Any given program costs more and takes longer.
>
> (3)   If a program is useful, it will have to be changed.
>
> (4)   Any given program will expand to fill all available memory.
>
> (5)   If a program is useless, it will be documented.
>
> (6)   The value of a program is proportional to the weight of its output.
>
> (7)   Program complexity grows until it exceeds the capability of the programmer who must maintain it.
>
> (8)   Make it possible for programmers to write programs in English, and you will find that programmers cannot write in English.

Flap's Law:

> Any inanimate object, regardless of its position or configuration, may be expected to perform at any time in a totally unexpected manner for reasons that are either entirely obscure or else completely mysterious.

Murphy's First Law:
>   Nothing is as easy as it looks.

Murphy's Second Law:
>   Everything takes longer than you think.

Murphy's Third Law:
>   In any field of scientific endeavor, anything that can go
>   wrong will go wrong.

Murphy's Fourth Law:
>   If there is a possibility of several things going wrong, the one
>   that will cause the most damage will be the one to go wrong.

Murphy's Fifth Law:
>   If anything just cannot go wrong, it will anyway.

Murphy's Sixth Law:
>   If you perceive that there are four possible ways in which a
>   procedure can go wrong and circumvent these, then a fifth
>   way, unprepared for, will promptly develop.

Murphy's Seventh Law:
>   Left to themselves, things tend to go from bad to worse.

Murphy's Eighth Law:
>   If everything seems to be going well, you have obviously
>   overlooked something.

Murphy's Ninth Law:
>   Nature always sides with the hidden flaw.

Murphy's Tenth Law:
>   Mother Nature is a bitch.

Murphy's Eleventh Law:

It is impossible to make anything foolproof, because fools are so ingenious.

Murphy's Law of Thermodynamics:

Things get worse under pressure.

Finagle's Rules:

Ever since the first scientific experiment, man has been plagued by the increasing antagonism of nature. It seems only right that nature should be logical and neat, but experience has shown that this is not the case. A further series of rules has been formulated, designed to help man accept the pigheadedness of nature:

(1) To study a subject best, understand it thoroughly before you start.

(2) Always keep a record of data. It indicates you've been working.

(3) Always draw your curves, then plot the reading.

(4) In case of doubt, make it sound convincing.

(5) Experiments should be reproducible. They should all fail in the same way.

(6) Do not believe in miracles. Rely on them.

(7) If an experiment works, something has gone wrong.

(8) No matter what result is anticipated, there will always be someone eager to (a) misinterpret it, (b) fake it, or (c) believe it happened to his own pet theory.

(9) In any collection of data, the figure most obviously correct, beyond all need of checking, is the mistake.

Corollary 1: No one whom you ask for help will see it.

Corollary 2: Everyone who stops by with unsought advice will see it immediately.

(10) Once a job is fouled up, anything done to improve it only makes it worse.

(11) Science is truth—don't be misled by facts.

Charley's Observation:

Computers were invented by Murphy.

Landau's Programming Paradoxes:

(1)   The world's best programmer has to be someone.

(2)   The more humanlike a computer becomes, the less it spends time computing and the more it spends time doing more humanlike work.

(3)   A software committee of one is limited by its own horizon and will specify software only that far.

(4)   When the system programmers declare the system works, it has worked and will work again some day.

Turnauckas' Law:

The attention span of a computer is only as long as its electrical cord.

The Law of Computerdom According to Golub:

(1)   Fuzzy project objectives are used to avoid the embarrassment of estimating the corresponding cost.

(2)   A carelessly planned project will take only twice as long.

(3)   The effort required to correct course increases geometrically with time.

(4)   Project teams detest weekly progress reporting because it so vividly manifests their lack of progress.

Blauw's Law:

Established technology tends to persist in spite of new technology.

Brook's Law:

Adding manpower to a late software project makes it later.

Hoare's Law of Large Programs:
Inside every large program is a small program struggling to get out.

The Law of Computability Applied to Social Sciences:
If at first you don't succeed, transform your data set.

The Ninety-Ninety Rule of Project Schedules:
The first 90 per cent of the tasks takes 10 per cent of the time and the last 10 per cent takes the other 90 per cent.

Wain's Conclusions:
(1)   He who gets too big for his britches, gets exposed in the end.
(2)   Staying afloat in management is easier if you don't make big waves.
(3)   The only people making money these days are the ones who sell computer paper.
(4)   If you didn't have problems, you wouldn't need people around to help solve them. Conversely, if you didn't have people around, maybe you wouldn't have problems.
(5)   Nothing motivates a man more than to see his boss putting in an honest day's work.
(6)   Bosses are so busy delegating jobs, they have no time to do any work.
(7)   When someone blows your horn, it sounds like a Cadillac. When you toot, it sounds like a Volkswagen.
(8)   You can tell some people aren't afraid of work by the way they fight it.
(9)   People who mind their own business succeed because they have so little competition.

Turnauckas' Observation:
To err is human; to really foul things up takes a computer.

Gib's Laws of Computer Unreliability:

(1)   Computers are unreliable, but humans are even more unreliable.

(2)   Any system which depends on human reliability is an unreliable system.

(3)   The only difference between the fool and the criminal who attack a system is that the fool attacks unpredictably and on a broader front.

(4)   Self-checking systems tend to have the inherent lack of reliability of the system in which they are used.

(5)   The error-detection and correction capabilities of any system will serve the key to understanding the type of error which they can not handle.

(6)   Undetectable errors are infinite in variety, in contrast to detectable errors, which by definition are limited.

(7)   Investment in reliability will increase until it exceeds the probable cost of errors or until somebody insists on getting some useful work done.

Bernetic's Law:

A doggone computer is man's best friend.

The Programmer's Nemesis:

Experts theorize that, through evolution and inbreeding, programmers may become a distinct subspecies of the human race.

The System Designer's Trouble:

All systems designed to be wonderfully efficient are hell for the people who supply the input and use the output.

Grosch's Law:

Computing power increases as the square of the cost. If you want to do it twice as cheaply, you have to do it four times as fast.

Isaac Asimov's Three Laws of Robotics:

(1)   A robot may not injure a human being or, through inaction, allow a human being to come to harm.

(2)   A robot must obey orders given to it by a human being except where such orders would conflict with the first law.

(3)   A robot must protect its own existence as long as such protection does not conflict with the first or second law.

Horowitz's Song for In-House Computer Programs:

"I/O, I/O, it's off to work we go . . ."

Horowitz's Rules:

(1)   Wisdom consists of knowing when to avoid perfection.

(2)   A computer makes as many mistakes in two seconds as twenty men working twenty years make.

(3)   There exist unthinkable thoughts.

Galef's Deductions:

(1)   Microminiaturization just makes the problem harder to get at.

(2)   Flaws found in the program will usually turn out to be flaws in the system, but never vice versa.

(3)   Fallible men design fallible computers.

Hunt's Law of Suspense:

If any work has a suspense date on it, that work will be completed as close to the suspense date as possible regardless of how far in advance the work was programmed.

A Law for the Future:

If it's not in a computer, it doesn't exist.

Utvich's Observation:

One accurate measurement is worth a thousand expert opinions.

Bassagordian's Basic Principle and Ultimate Axiom:
> By definition, when you are investigating the unknown, you do not know what you will find or even when you have found it.

Einstein Theory of Relatives:
> The number of person's relatives is directly proportional to his fame.

McAuley's Axiom:
> If a system is of sufficient complexity, it will be built before it is designed, implemented before it is tested, and outdated before it is debugged.

Clarke's Laws:
> (1)   When a distinguished, but elderly scientist states that something is possible, he is almost certainly right. When he states that something is impossible, he is very probably wrong.
>
> (2)   The only way to discover the limits of the possible is to look beyond them into the impossible.
>
> (3)   Any sufficiently advanced technology is indistinguishable from magic.

Maier's Laws:
> (1)   If facts do not conform to the theory, they must be disposed of.
>
> (2)   The bigger the theory, the better.

Another One of Murphy's Laws:
> If mathematically you end up with the incorrect answer, try multiplying by the page number.

Snafu Equations:

(1)   Given any problem containing n equations, there will be $n+1$ unknowns.

(2)   An object or bit of information most needed will be least available.

(3)   Any device requiring service or adjustment will be least accessible.

(4)   Interchangeable devices won't.

(5)   Badness comes in waves.

Bradley's Bromide:

If computers get too powerful, we can organize them into committee. That'll do them in.

The Engineer's Law:

If it can't be done with jumpers, it isn't worth doing.

Arthur C. Clarke's Law:

It has yet to be proven that intelligence has any survival value.

The Fail-Safe Theorem:

When a fail-safe system fails, it fails by failing to be fail-safe.

Fahrguard's Four Laws of Thermodynamics:

(1)   No matter how hard you try, you can only break even.

(2)   You can only break even at absolute zero.

(3)   Absolute zero is impossible to attain.

(4)   No matter how hard you shake it, the last few drops always run down your pants.

Rabinow's Observation:

The road to the patent office is paved with good inventions.

Launegayer's Maxim:

All the world's an analog stage, and digital circuits play only bit parts.

Walder's Observation:

A mathematician is one who is willing to assume everything except responsibility.

Featherstone's Accurate Steps to Systems Development:

(1)   Wild enthusiasm.
(2)   Disillusionment.
(3)   Total confusion.
(4)   Search for the guilty.
(5)   Punishment of the innocent.
(6)   Promotion of nonparticipants.

Klipstein's Rules for General Engineering:

(1)   A patent application will be preceded by one week by a similar application made by an independent worker.
(2)   The more innocuous a design change appears to be, the further its influence will extend.
(3)   All warranty and guarantee clauses become void upon payment of the invoice.

Valery's Definition:

Science is a collection of successful recipes.

Galileo's Conclusion:

Science proceeds more by what it has learned to ignore than what it takes into account.

Howe's Law:

Every man has a scheme that won't work.

Weinberg's Law:

> If builders built buildings the way the programmers wrote programs, the first woodpecker that came along would destroy civilization.

Neville's Conclusion:

> Research is a straight line from the tangent of a well-known assumption to the center of a foregone conclusion.

Horgan's Homily:

> We won't have personal computing until we can get them little and talking.

The Ordering Principle:

> Those supplies necessary for yesterday's experiment must be ordered no later than tomorrow noon.

☞ "WELL, THAT'S LIFE" SECTION OF APHORISMS

Harvey's Homily:
    A man's brain is his Achilles' heel.

Campbell's Principle:
    He who hoots with the owl at night will not soar with the
    eagle at dawn.

Newman's Law:
    Hypocrisy is the Vaseline of social intercourse.

Today's School Graduate's Words for Starting a Conversation:
    "You know . . ."

Johnson-Laird's Law:
    Toothaches tend to occur on Saturday nights.

Kopcha's Rule:
    There is always one more son of a bitch than you counted
    on.

Newton's First Law:
    Some days it's better to stay in bed.

Luebbert's Law:
    Liars get caught by the tale.

Gregory's Observations:

(1)   Popularity almost always leads to deterioration in quality.

(2)   A belief is of no value until you can defend it rationally against all comers.

(3)   When a man becomes so busy that he forgets the beautiful things in life, then it can be truly said he is poor.

O'Malley's Conclusion:

Life is a series of movements from one chair to another.

Barker's Byword:

When you are over the hill, you pick up speed.

A Fireside Observation:

God still seems to be helping those who take a big helping for themselves.

The "Where Are They When You Need Them?" Principle:

If a man steals from you once, he's a fool; if a man steals from you twice, you're the fool; if he steals from you thrice, the odds are eight to five the thief and the agency charged with the theft protection are one and the same.

Gerhardt's Law:

If you find something you like, buy a lifetime supply—they're going to stop making it.

Old French Proverb:

The barrel always smells of herring.

Humiston's Law:

When you are up to your ass in alligators, it is hard to remember that your original intention was to drain the swamp.

Allan's Axiom:

> Supersonic travel means that although you still can't be in two places at once, at least you can be heard trying over a wide area.

Haver's Law:

> A drunken man's words are a somber man's thoughts.

Riley's Rumination:

> Don't let anyone kid you about the life of Riley.

Lael's Law:

> Hindsight is always 20/20.

Kegley's Principle of Observation:

> No matter where or what, there are makers, takers, and fakers.

Grandpa's Law:

> Any jackass can kick down a barn, but it takes a good carpenter to build one.

Nick the Greek's Law of Life:

> All things considered, life is 9 to 5 against.

Edwinn's Corollary:

> People with money live so damn long.

Cavanaugh's Postulate:

> All the kookies are not in the jar.

Preston's Laws:

(1) Two's company, three's an orgy.

(2) All the world loves a four-letter word.

(3) Genius is 10 per cent inspiration and 50 per cent capital gains.

Stock's Observation:

You no sooner get your head above water than someone pulls your flippers off.

Schmidt's Observation:

All things being equal, a fat person uses more soap than a thin person.

Grandma Soderquist's Observation:

A road map always tells you everything except how to refold it.

Sousa's Observation:

Some instruments in a drum-and-bugle corps are purely cymbolic.

Renau's Rural Rule:

If your cow doesn't give milk, sell him.

Fractured Franklinism:

A bird in the hand is worth about three Kleenex.

Si Perkins' "People Differ" Law:

Some object to the fan dancer, others to the fan.

Brown's Bromide:

A "peace-loving nation" is one which bans fireworks and makes hydrogen bombs.

The Law of Divine Intervention:

Alle Kunst ist umsunst
Wenn ein Engel auf das
Zündloch brunzt. (German version)
All skill is in vain when an angel pees in the touchhole of your musket. (English translation)

Boone's Forest Observation:
> Porcupines prick.

Puritan's First Law:
> Evil is "live" spelled backward.

Puritan's Second Law:
> If it feels good, don't do it.

Ponsy's Postulate:
> By the time a man can read a woman like a book, he is too old to collect a library.

Launegayer's Axiom:
> Pound for pound, the amoeba is the most vicious animal on earth.

The Circe Axiom:
> Lust makes the world go round.

Wolfe's Translation:
> *E pluribus unum* (anything for a buck).

The "Enough Already" Law:
> The more you run over a dead cat, the flatter it gets.

Leon's Liquor Law:
> Work is the curse of the drinking man.

Allen's Conclusion:
> Betty Crocker uses a mix.

Allen's Maxim:
> God must love stupid people, He made so many of them.

Grandma Soderquist's Rumination:
> Some people fish in the Sea of Life without bait.

Kassorla's Safe-Distance Axiom:
> When walking a dog, be sure the animal is smaller than you.

Rev. Patrick Mahaffy's Observation:
> There's no such thing as a large whiskey.

The Postman's Theory:
> Everything in a plain brown wrapper is dirty.

The Law of Comparative Pleasure:
> Sex: even when it's bad, it's good.

Agnes' Law:
> Almost everything in life is easier to get into than out of.

Dan Green's Rule:
> What the large print giveth, the small print taketh away.

Ahlskog's Axiom:
> Half of life's experiences are below average in satisfaction.

Merrill's First Corollary:
> There are no winners in life; only survivors.

Browning's Theorem:
> Less is more.

Pastore's Comment on Browning's Theorem:
> Nothing is ultimate.

Samuel Butler's Law:
> Life is one long process of getting tired.

Drew's Law:
Life is full of minor and major problems; some days you get
both.

Van Roy's Truisms:
> (1) Life is a whole series of circumstances beyond your control.
>
> (2) There has been only one indispensable man . . . ADAM.

The Dirty-Old-Man Axiom:
> The number of women a man finds attractive is truely proportionate to his age.

Grandma Soderquist's Conclusion:
> The honeymoon is over when the one-holer outhouse is made into a two-holer.

The Law of Selective Gravity, or the Buttered-Side-Down Law:
> An object will fall so as to do the most damage.

Newton's Little Known Seventh Law:
> A bird in the hand is safer than one over head.

Utvich's Wisdom:
> A born loser is a guy who loses even in his fantasies.

J. B. Stearn's Homily:
> Success is like a fart—only your own smells good.

Swipple's Rule of Order:
> He who shouts loudest has the floor.

Houde's Rumination:
> A martyr is a hero who didn't make it.

The Beautiful-Princess Law:
> Before you meet any handsome prince, you have to kiss a lot of toads.

Leibenguth's Law:
>A cynic is but an honorable man with experience.

Freeman's Law:
>Halitosis is better than no breath at all.

Greeniaus' Observation:
>History tailgates.

The Over-the-Hill Law:
>At the age fifty you've got it made; you can coast in—it's down hill all the way.

Dr. Johnson's Law of Sexual Satisfaction:
>The only time you've had enough is when you've just finished.

O. O. McIntyre's Law:
>There is no such thing as a "little bit of garlic."

Colby's Observations:
>(1) Some men are legends in their own mind.
>(2) Bigotry doesn't have a Chinaman's chance.
>(3) The secret of eternal youth: don't mellow.
>(4) "Leisured" does not mean "leisurely."

An Old Middle East Proverb:
>A friend advises in his interest, not yours.

Askerberg's Axiom:
>You win some, you lose some, and some get rained out, but you gotta suit up for them all.

Carson's Law:

It's better to be rich and healthy than poor and sick.

A Psychological Truism:

>No man is lonely while eating spaghetti—it requires so much attention.

Mobil's Maxim:

>Bad regulation begets worse regulation.

Cole's Law:

>Thinly sliced cabbage.

Pardo's Postulates:

>(1)   Anything good is either illegal, immoral, or fattening.
>
>(2)   The three faithful things in life are money, a dog, and an old woman.
>
>(3)   Don't care if you're rich or not, as long as you can live comfortably and have everything you want.

Dalton's Truism:

>Life is a series of incomplete passes.

A Mother's Law:

>Happiness is a warm puppy with an empty bladder.

Moer's Truism:

>The trouble with most jobs is the job holder's resemblance to being one of a sled-dog team. No one gets a change of scenery, except the lead dog.

Long's Notes:

>Climate is what you expect.

A "Lucky Strike" Rule:

>Lighting a cigarette after siphoning gas can be injurious to your health.

Sturgeon's Law:

> Ninety per cent of everything is crud.

Dietvorst's Law:

> You climb the ladder of success easier when you lay it flat.

Laver's Law:

> The same dress can be known as "indecent" ten years before its time, "daring" a year before its time. Then it becomes "chic" and in two or three years, "dowdy." It is considered "hideous" twenty years later, "quaint" in thirty years, and a hundred and a hundred and fifty years later it is "beautiful."

Hodge's Homily:

    There comes a time in a man's life when he must rise above principle.

Cann's Axiom:

    When all else fails, read the instructions.

Malinowski's Law:

    Looking from far above, from our high places of safety in the developed civilization, it is easy to see all the crudity and irrelevance of magic.

Sammy Davis, Jr.'s Dictum:

    A professional is one who does a good job even when he doesn't feel like it.

Dr. Reyer's Reflection:

    Losing makes winning worthwhile.

Van Roy's Law:

    Honesty is the best policy—there's less competition.

Malkin's Rule:

    The more things you own, the more you are owned by things.

Van Roy's Axiom:
> The trouble with people is their trouble with people.

Litzler's Law of International Travel:
> Never, ever, fly on the airline of the country from which you are departing.

Honoré de Balzac's Conclusion:
> There is only one giant machine operated by pygmies, and that is a bureaucracy.

Laocoön's Law of Improbable Generosity:
> Don't look a gift horse in the mouth, but do check for Greek soldiers elsewhere in its anatomy.

Filson's Law:
> "Push" is the force exerted upon the door marked PULL.

Grandma Soderquist's Thought:
> There are those who don't even like to be rubbed the right way.

Bersani's Law:
> If someone says, "I'm expensive"—believe them.

Van Roy's Truism:
> If you can tell the difference between good advice and bad advice, you don't need advice.

Charles de Gaulle's Postulate:
> The graveyards are full of indispensable men.

Ralph's Observation:
> It is a mistake to allow any mechanical object to realize you are in a hurry.

Kramer's Law:

    You can never tell which way the train went by looking at the track.

Emil Freireich's Law:

> General solutions to specific problems become specific problems requiring general solutions.

Louis's Logic:

> One and one does not necessarily make 11.

Mueller's Law:

> You only have a problem if you think it is a problem.

The Feather-Bed Law:

> Success is just a matter of pluck.

Preston's Axiom:

> Never put off till tomorrow what you can avoid all together.

Le Châtelier's Law:

> If some stress is brought to bear on a system in equilibrium, the equilibrium is displaced in the direction which tends to undo the effect of the stress.

Feldman's Law:

> Don't lie, steal, or cheat unnecessarily.

Hartley's First Law:

> You can lead a horse to water, but if you can get him to float on his back—you've got something.

Linus Pauling's Rumination:

> The best way to have a good idea is to have a lot of ideas.

Sevareid's Law:

> The chief cause of problems is solutions.

Grandma Soderquist's Truism:

> Most pigs end up making hogs of themselves.

A Don Quixote Quote:

> Beware, gentle knight—the greatest monster of them all is reason.

Manly's Maxim:

> Logic is a systematic method of coming to the wrong conclusion with confidence.

MacWhinney's Observation:

> What some people lack in intelligence, they more than make up for in stupidity.

Westfield's Law of Job Seeking:

> Never sell more of yourself than you can later buy back with skill and performance.

Jaeger's Facts:

> (1) Co-operation is doing with a smile that which you have to do anyway.
>
> (2) It's known fact—cross-eyed teachers cannot control their pupils.
>
> (3) Tell a man there are 300 billion stars in the universe and he'll believe you. Tell him a bench has wet paint on it and he'll have to touch to be sure.
>
> (4) Use your head—it's the little things that count.
>
> (5) An idea is a curious thing. It will not work unless you do.
>
> (6) When success turns a man's head, it usually turns everyone else's stomach.
>
> (7) There is a difference between an open mind and a hole in the head.

Doyle's Law of Ones:

> If you can be off by one, you will be.

Bustlin' Billy's Bogus Beliefs:

> (1) The organization of any program reflects the organization of the people who develop it.
>
> (2) A little humility is arrogance.
>
> (3) History proves nothing.
>
> (4) A lot of what appears to be progress is just so much technological rococo.
>
> (5) There is nòthing so unbecoming on the beach as a wet kilt.
>
> (6) Capitalism can exist in only one of two states—welfare or warfare.
>
> (7) Anything is possible, but nothing is easy.

Truths of Management:

> (1) Think before you act; it's not your money.
>
> (2) Good management is the expression of one great idea.
>
> (3) No executive ever devotes any effort to proving himself wrong.
>
> (4) Cash in must exceed cash out.
>
> (5) Management capability is always less than the organization actually needs.
>
> (6) Either an executive can do his job, or he can't.
>
> (7) If sophisticated calculations are needed to justify an action, don't do it.
>
> (8) If you are doing something wrong, you will do it badly.
>
> (9) If you are attempting the impossible, you will fail.
>
> (10) The easiest way of making money is to stop losing it.

La Rochefoucauld's Law:

> A kind heart is of little value in chess.

Sparks's Law of Problem Solution:

 The chances of solving a problem decline the closer one gets to finding out who was the cause of the problem.

Hobson's Homily:

 Common sense is the least common of all senses.

Shanahan's Law:

 The length of any meeting rises with the square of the number of people present.

Fox's Philosophy:

 The most intelligent people we know are those who ask advice.

Greenberg's First Law of Experts:

 You don't ever ask a barber whether you need a haircut.

Edison's Axiom:

 We don't know one millionth of 1 per cent about anything.

Thompson's Adage:

 Be kind. Remember everyone you meet is fighting a hard battle.

Allison's Precept:

 The best simple-minded test of expertise in a particular area is the ability to win money in a series of bets on future occurrences in that area.

Philosopher's Principle:

 It is more shameful to distrust one's friends than to be deceived by them.

Army Axiom:

Any order that can be misunderstood has been misunderstood.

Baehr's Conclusions:

    (1)   Never get into a pissing contest with a skunk.

    (2)   Grab them by the balls; the hearts and minds will follow.

Pareto's Law:

    Twenty per cent of the customers account for 80 per cent of the turnover, 20 per cent of components account for 80 per cent of the cost, and so forth.

G. K. Chesterton's Observation:

    I have seen the truth, and it makes no sense.

Finley Peter Dunne's Credo:

    Trust everybody; but always cut the cards.

Boren's Laws:

    (1)   When in doubt, mumble.

    (2)   When in trouble, delegate.

    (3)   When in charge, ponder.

Nowlan's Theory:

    He who hesitates is not only lost, but several miles from the next freeway exit.

Long's Notes:

    (1)   Never underestimate the power of human stupidity.

    (2)   Beware of altruism. It is based on self-deception, the root of all evil.

The Duke of Windsor's Two Greatest Pieces of Advice:

    Never refuse a chance to sit down or an opportunity to relieve yourself.

Saunder's Slants:

    (1)   As scarce as the truth is, the supply is much greater than the demand.

    (2)   Whose bread I eat, his song I sing.

    (3)   If it's worth doing, it is worth hiring someone who knows how to do it.

    (4)   There is always free cheese in a mousetrap.

    (5)   The expedient thing and the right thing are seldom the same thing.

The Law of Predicted Results:

    Market research can be conducted and interpreted to prove any desired conclusion.

Cheop's Law:

    Nothing ever gets built on schedule or within budget.

Peers's Law:

    The solution to a problem changes the nature of the problem.

Sattinger's Law:

    It works better if you plug it in.

Feldstein's Law:

    Never, ever, play leapfrog with a unicorn.

The Golden Rule:

    Whoever has the gold makes the rules.

The Point-of-No-Return Law:

    The light at the end of the tunnel could turn out to be the headlight of an oncoming train.

Westheimer's Rule:

    To estimate the time it takes to do a task, estimate the time you think it should take, multiply by 2, and change the unit of measure to the next highest unit. Thus we allocate two days for a one-hour task.

Samuel Johnson's Rule:

There are few ways in which a man can be more innocently employed than in making money.

Leo Rosten's Law:

Second-rate people hire third-rate people.

Dickerson's Truism:

"Off the top of the head" ideas are often like dandruff—small and flaky.

Poirier's Comment:

Procrastination, like all other long words, is the thief of time.

Kangnekar's Modified Rules Concerning Decisions:

(1)   If you must make a decision, delay it.

(2)   If you can authorize someone else to avoid a decision, do so.

(3)   If you can form a committee, have them avoid the decision.

(4)   If you can otherwise avoid a decision, avoid it immediately.

Peter's Placebo:

An ounce of image is worth a pound of performance.

Eddy's Old Chinese Proverb:

He who never sticks out neck, never wins by nose.

The Attorney's Rule:

If the facts are against you, argue the law. If the law is against you, pound the table and yell like hell.

Ben Franklin's Observation:

A full belly makes a full brain.

Cohen's Law:
> What really matters is the name you succeed in imposing on the facts—not the facts themselves.

Retail Buyer's Motto:
> Never underestimate the lack of taste of the buying public.

Pate's Postulate:
> A bird in the hand is too small for dinner (or the bush may taste better anyway).

The Hidden Truth of Management:
> Kickbacks must always exceed bribes.

Tuccille's First Law of Reality:
> Industry always moves in to fill an economic vacuum.

Roberts' Rule:
> At no time in history of mankind have there been enough important executive positions available for all the important people alive at the time.

Stale's Law:
> No matter how careful one is in resealing the inner liner in cereal boxes, it will tear where it is glued to the box.

Cavanaugh's Discovery:
> Never, ever, enter a battle of wits half-armed.

Shomaker's Laws:
> (1) All companies experience corporate menopause.
> (2) An intelligent person can make a dumber statement than an idiot. The idiot is limited to his imbecility.

The Employment Rule:
> A company is known by the company it employs.

☞ No List Is Complete Without Some Sexually Oriented Stuff

The Rueful Bachelor's Law:
> There is no such thing as an unattached woman.

Fortis' Three Great Lies in Life:
    (1)   Money isn't everything.
    (2)   It's great to be born in a ghetto.
    (3)   I'm only going to put it in a little way.

King Solomon's Law for 500th Wife:
> It's going to be plenty soft for you.

Johnny Carson's Observation on Geriatrics:
> Sex in the sixties is great, but it improves if you pull over to the side of the road.

Dr. Stolfa's Three Great Happinesses of Life:
    (1)   Breaking wind in church and sitting in own phew.
    (2)   A martini before and a cigarette afterward.
    (3)   Coming.

Grandma Soderquist's Observation:
> More farm families got their start in the hayloft than ever did in the farmhouse.

The Singles Club Law:
> If computer dating fails, just trust to lust.

Dean's Law:

> Better to have flunked your Wasserman, than never to have loved at all.

The New-Product Syndrome:

> The longer you sleep with your dream girl, the harder it is to kiss her good-by.

The Shrink's Assessment:

> There's no point in worrying about apathy when you can't care less.

Bula's Basic Belief:

> "Love for Sale" may not be a bad song title, but in commerce, it would constitute a misrepresentation of services.

Kelley's Observations:

> (1) There's one major difference between the modern girl and her mother—the former goes ahead and does what the latter always wanted to do.
>
> (2) Dancing is wonderful training for girls. It's the first way they learn to guess what a man is going to do before he does it.

Larkin's Law:

> Sex is only dirty—if it's done right.

Zall's Law:

> A dirty book is seldom dusty.

Westlake's Sage Remark:

> Love is never having to say how much.

Brandstadt's Observation:

> Sin now—pray later.

Billings' Notes:
> (1) Sex has no calories.
>
> (2) Infants don't have as much fun in infancy as adults do in adultery.
>
> (3) A dirty old man is just a sexually active senior citizen.
>
> (4) Kissing a man without a mustache is like eating an egg without salt.

Kesell's Law:
> If a man writes a better book, preaches a better sermon, or beds a better whore than his neighbor, though he builds his domicile deep in the woods, the world will beat a path to his door to find out who the better whore was.

Bula's Truism:
> Love and marriage go together like a horse and carriage, so the sooner we get these obsolete forms of transport back, the better.

The Birth-Control Law:
> If a birth control device is going to fail, it will do so on the thirteenth or fourteenth day between two given periods.

Steiner's Statement:
> Both business and love require the temperament of a vampire combined with the discretion of an anemone.

The Nudist Colony Rule:
> Folks playing leapfrog must complete all jumps.

Clarke's Conclusion:
> Never let your sense of morals interfere with doing the right thing.

Hart's Homily:
Virginity can be cured.

An Italian Proverb:
> She who is silent consents.

Draper's Law:
> A bachelor can only chase a girl until she catches him.

The "Just Say No" Law:
> Don't be a girl who gives long explanations as to why she "doesn't"—or before you're done explaining, you'll wind up one who "does."

Frank's Law:
> Sex is a misdemeanor—the more you miss, da' meaner you get.

Hayden's Homilies:
> (1) No matter how much cats fight, there are always plenty of kittens.
> (2) Insanity might be inherited—you get if from your kids.
> (3) No one should boast of his integrity until he has a good chance to be dishonest.
> (4) You can become so accustomed to tension that when things get calm, you become nervous.
> (5) Love is like hash—you have to have confidence in it before you enjoy it.
> (6) Success is getting what you want. Happiness is wanting what you get.

Borland's Postulates:
> (1) Birth control is avoiding the issue.
> (2) The streetwalker's dog is a whore hound.

Van's Conclusions:

> (1)   Marriage vows: promise to love, honor, and stimulate the economy.
>
> (2)   Two's company and three's the result.
>
> (3)   Concerning love-making: in the thirties it was the rumble seat, in the forties the back seat, in the fifties the reclining front seat, in the sixties the camper, and in the seventies—it's where ever the mood strikes.

Mark's Mark:

> Love is a matter of chemistry; sex is a matter of physics.

Miller's Law:

> You cannot tell how deep a puddle is until you step in it.

Barlow's Nature Thoughts:

> (1)   Most fish shyly swish, but jellyfish can only squish.
>
> (2)   Turtles never hurtle.

Oler's Apothegm:

> The genuineness of a couple's affection for each other is inversely proportional to the cuteness of their pet names for each other.

Van Roy's Postulate:

> Love is like a pair of socks—you have to have two, and they gotta match.

Korman's Conclusion:

> The trouble with resisting temptation is it may never come again.

☞ Some Steppingstones for Backpackers, Students of Life, and Agronomists

Forde's Law:

No matter which way you spit, it's up wind.

Knight's Law:

Life is what happens to you while you're making other plans.

The Law of Inverse Appreciation:

The less there is between you and the environment, the more you appreciate the environment.

Russell's Observation:

Due to a lack of trained trumpeters, the end of the world has been postponed indefinitely.

Long's Notes:

Climate is what you expect. Weather is what you get.

Thomaseen's Adam-and-Eve Truism:

The human race was not really created—it is solely a fig leaf of our imagination.

Walther's Warning:

Never believe that a package of pitted dates has no pits.

Barber's Laws of Backpacking:

(1) The integral of the gravitational potential taken around any loop trail you choose to hike always comes positive.

(2) Any stone in your boot always migrates against the pressure gradient to exactly the point of most pressure.

(3) The weight of your pack increases in direct proportion to the amount of food you consume from it. If you run out of food, the pack weight goes on increasing anyway.

(4) The number of stones in your boot is directly proportional to the number of hours you've been on the trail.

(5) The difficulty of finding any given trail marker is directly proportional to the importance of the consequences of failing to find it.

(6) The size of each of the stones in your boot is directly proportional to the number of hours you've been on the trail.

(7) The remaining distance to your chosen campsite remains constant as twilight approaches.

(8) The net weight of your boots is proportional to the cube of the number of hours you have been on the trail.

(9) When you arrive at your chosen campsite, it is full.

(10) If you take your boots off, you'll never get them back on.

(11) The local density of mosquitoes is inversely proportional to your remaining repellent.

Ferris' Frothing:

Man has less tenacity than crab·grass.

Long's Truism:

Natural laws have no pity.

Charles Beard's Summarizations of History:

(1) The bee fertilizes the flower it robs.

(2) When it is dark enough, you can see the stars.

Mangravite's Postulate:

There are no absolute answers to life—just revelations.

The Law of Archaeological Analysis:

One stone is a stone; two stones are a feature; three stones are a wall.

Bruce's Cogent Comments:

(1)   Best meal I ever put in my whole mouth.

(2)   Everybody in the room was there.

(3)   The lake comes right up to the shore.

Hufstader's Insight:

Time is nature's way of keeping everything from happening at once.

The Weather-Report Rule:

Bad weather reports are more often right than good ones.

Defalque's Observation:

A path without obstacles probably leads nowhere.

The First Law of Bicycling:

No matter which way you ride, it's up hill and against the wind.

The First Law of Canoeing:

No matter which direction you start, it's always against the wind coming back.

The Land-Use Principle of Conservation:

Thou shalt not rape the land, for that shall be known as "Sodomy."

Wilner's Observation:

> All conversations with a potato should be conducted in private.

Bradshaw's Further Adventures in Backpacking:

> (1)   Backpackers don't get lost—they just get disoriented.
> (2)   When eliminating unnecessary equipment before a trip, the first thing you decide not to take will be the first thing you need on the hike.

Byrne's Law:

> A bird in the hand betokens mutual trust.

Grandma Soderquist's Conclusion:

> A chicken doesn't stop scratching just because the worms are scarce.

Ponsy's Postulate:

> Faith is the bird that sings while it is still dark.

The "Stay Cool" Rule:

> You cannot sink someone else's end of the boat and still keep your own afloat.

Hill's Hard-and-Fast Rules of Survival:

> (1)   Never play cards with a horse trader who'll bet his sweet ass.
> (2)   Beware of the doctor whose wife sells cemetery lots, whose brother owns a granite quarry, and whose father deals in spades.
> (3)   Do not trust a veterinarian with the nickname "Bones."

Match's Maxim:
> A fool in a high station is like a man on the top of a high mountain: everything appears small to him and he appears small to everybody.

Rhoda's Rumination:
> It's always darkest before it's pitch black.

The Skier's Rumination:
> Don't ever eat yellow snow.

Graebner's Sage Comment:
> If you eat beans when camping, leave your sleeping bag unzipped.

Merill's Second Corollary:
> In the highway of life, the average happening is of about as much true significance as a dead skunk in the middle of the road.

Nancy's Belief:
> God didn't create the world in seven days, He screwed around for six and pulled an all-nighter.

Borland's Postulate:
> Beginning rock hounds take everything for granite.

Grandma Sonderquist's Riposte:
> The worms start multiplying when the chickens stop scratching.

Sir Edmund Hillary's Conclusion:
> Mountain climbers always help each other.

John Bear's Observations:
    (1)   Little things come in small packages.
    (2)   Mistakes are the steppingstones to failure.
    (3)   A silent man does not always know a secret.
    (4)   The best offense is a strong offense.
    (5)   It is not necessary to fall into a well to know its depth.
    (6)   Soon ripe, soon rotten.
    (7)   Ambition plagues the inarticulate hardest.
    (8)   The longest list has a final item.

The Poverty Principle:
    Money is like manure—it is meant to be spread around.

Call's Law of Frustration:
    The measure of a bird dog's intelligence can be determined by the length of time it takes to resign yourself to his way of thinking.

Call's Law of Negative Results:
    The distance from a flushed covey is directly proportional to the number of fellow hunters you and your dog are trying to impress.

Daniel's Doodle:
    Man who slings mud, loses ground.

Lorene's Law:
    A bird in the hand—may pee.

Mark Twain's Observation:
    Part of the secret of success in life is to eat what you like and let the food fight it out inside.

The Home Gardener's Law:
    A green thumb is a lot of manure.

Van Roy's Laws:

(1) College is a fountain of knowledge where students come to drink.

(2) Don't wear ear muffs in a land of rattlesnakes.

(3) The man who invented the eraser had the human race pretty well sized up.

Loewen's Law:

The worm in the sour apple doesn't know any better.

Mark Twain's thought:

Man is the only animal that blushes. Or needs to.

Epstean's Law:

If self-preservation is the first of law of life, exploitation is the second.

Dr. Finklestein's Rules on Camping:

(1) If a sight is worth seeing, someone will build a highway to it.

(2) If you can afford a hotel, you need not sleep in a tent.

(3) When you camp on a cold day, you will be faced with colder night.

Hugo's Rules of Life:

(1) Brute force, clumsiness, ignorance, and superstition will always triumph over science, skill, knowledge, and logic.

(2) Keep your eye on the ball, your shoulder to the wheel, your ear to the ground. Now, try to work in that position.

(3) DO IT TOMORROW—you've made enough mistakes today.

(4) Bulls and bears make money, but pigs lose their shirts.

(5) Old chemists never die; they just fail to react.

(6) If you can't be right—at least be careful.

Joe's Sage Thoughts:

(1)   No wonder the country is in a mess—half the people are below median intelligence.

(2)   Many of us combine the wisdom of youth with the energy of old age.

(3)   There's a new manual out on how to be spontaneous.

☞ TRUISMS FOR THAT DIRECTORS' MEETING

The Mutual-Fund Principle:
> Managers function (in certain situations) to hold gains to less than the market while assuring accelerated losses.

Kelley's Law:
> An executive will always return to work from lunch early if no one takes him.

George Bernard Shaw's Conclusion:
> If all the economists in the world were laid end to end, they still wouldn't reach a conclusion.

Robinson's Observation Regarding Consumption:
> In this day and age of rampant consumption, we seem to be expending increasing amounts of energy in every form except "individual."

Dr. Samuelson's Reflection:
> The real objective of a committee is not to reach a decision, but to avoid it.

Barton's Promotional Observation:
> America's No. 1 problem is that Madison Avenue runs the wrong way.

Ancient Roman Advice:
> *Illegitimus non Carborundum* (don't let the bastards grind you down).

Graham's Pronouncement, or The Basic Law of Budgets:
> You can only spend it once.

Brien's First Law:
> At some time in the life cycle of virtually every organization, its ability to succeed in spite of itself runs out.

Firestone's Principle of Investment Timing:
> The best investment opportunities are encountered when you are broke.

Boss Pogue's Observation:
> My men give their talent to our company and their genius to their expense accounts.

Turley's Lament:
> The first loss is the easiest.

Litzler's Law of Competitive Bidding:
> The bigger the specification, the lower the profit.

Allen's Observation:
> A consultant may be defined as an unemployed practitioner.

Steiger's Law:
> This is as bad as the situation can get—but don't bet on it.

The Product-Meets-These-Requirements Rule:
> If Detroit makes it, it must be an automobile.

The Systems Paradox:
> People in systems do not do what the systems say they are doing.

Mark Twain's Classic:
> Put all your eggs in one basket and—WATCH THAT BAS-KET.

Sharp's Solid Thinking:
> Crystal balls aren't really very productive.

Forde's Second Law:
> You can't win them all, but you can sure lose them all.

Forde's Third Law:
> The longer the letter, the less chance of its being read.

Launegayer's Observation:
> Asking dumb questions is easier than correcting dumb mistakes.

Moch's Theories for Spreading Executive Responsibility:
> (1) Note and initial.
> (2) See me and discuss.
> (3) Let's get together on this.
> (4) Give us the benefit of your thinking.
> (5) Let's take a survey [we need more time to think of an answer].
> (6) For your consideration [you hold the bag for awhile].
> (7) Take under advisement [ignore and hope everyone will forget it].

Kesell's Cardinal Principles of Leadership:
> (1) Career defense [cover your ass].
> (2) Verbal containment [shut your mouth].
> (3) Competition elimination [screw your buddies].

Newberry's Observation:

>The universal aptitude for ineptitude makes any human accomplishment an incredible miracle.

Somerset Maughan's Thought:

>Only a mediocre person is always at his best.

A Jason Rainbow Thought:

>Many of us believe that wrongs aren't wrong if it's done by nice people like ourselves.

Henderickson's Law:

>If you have enough meetings over a long period of time, the meetings become more important than the problem the meetings were intended to solve.

Cohen's Law:

>Everyone knows that the name of the game is what label you succeed in imposing on the facts.

Berkowitz's Postulate:

>A clean desk gives a sense of relief and a plan for impending disaster.

The Truth of Management:

>Organizations always have too many managers.

John's Law:

>In planning any corporate design, the most important variable is the age of the president's son.

Fudge's Law:

>If your answer and the prof's answer do not match, you have obviously left out the fudge factor.

Balfour's Declaration:

> Nothing matters very much in life, and very few things matter at all.

Kirkland's Law:

> The usefulness of any meeting is in inverse proportion to the attendance.

Quade's Law:

> In human relations the easiest thing to achieve is a misunderstanding.

The Secret-of-Success Law:

> Discover all unpredictable errors before they occur.

Mosher's Law:

> It's better to retire too soon than too late.

Nef's Law:

> There's a solution to every problem; the only difficulty is finding it.

The Numbers Maxim:

> Figures rarely lie; liars frequently figure.

Doelger's Thoughts:

> (1) Forecasting is a difficult thing—especially when it deals with the future.
> (2) If you're not rejected at least three times a week, you're not really trying.
> (3) A leap beyond the state of the art may be into a bucket of worms.

Weber's Law:
> Too many decisions are measured with a micrometer, marked with chalk, and cut with an ax.

Beau Jacques's Theorem of Personnel Management:
> Beware of the employee heralded as a man ahead of his time; on Wednesday he'll be wishing it was Friday.

Peter's Principle:
> In every hierarchy, whether it be government or business, each employee tends to rise to his level of incompetence; every post tends to be filled by an employee incompetent to execute its duties.

Peter's Corollaries:
> (1)   Incompetence knows no barriers of time or place.
> (2)   Work is accomplished by those employees who have not yet reached their level of incompetence.
> (3)   If at first you don't succeed, try something else.

Senator James Hamilton Lewis's Observation:
> One man plus courage is a majority.

Mrs. Truman's Corollary:
> The amount of heat in the kitchen is directly proportional to the amount of fire in the attic.

The Fifty-Sixth Vice President's Thought:
> Reform always comes from below. No man with four aces asks for a new deal.

Heller's Law:
> The first myth of management is that it exists.

Bula's Basic Laws:

(1)   A little knowledge is a dangerous thing. This explains the assured future of the security blanket, in all its forms.

(2)   The pen is mightier than the sword, but you must have money in the bank to back up that check.

(3)   Ginsberg's only hope: if you can't win, break even, or even quit the game, scheme to alter the rules.

Hunt's Rumination:

The one sitting, contributing nothing, is a supervisor.

Post's Postulate:

Power, like virtue, is its own reward.

The Iron Law of Distribution:

Them that has gits.

The IBM Pollyanna Principle:

Machines should work. People should think.

McFadden's Truism:

A committee is a group that keeps minutes and wastes hours.

Steiner's Philosophical Observations:

(1)   In business, as well as in chess, the winner is the one who makes the next to last mistake.

(2)   At business meetings the one unmatched asset is the ability to yawn with your mouth closed.

(3)   Consistency is the last refuge of the unimaginative.

(4)   Trivial matters take up more time because we know more about them than important matters.

Van Roy's Postulates:

(1)   He who hesitates is bossed.

(2)   A meeting is no substitute for progress.

(3)   It isn't who you know, it's who you "yes."

(4)   The wheels of progress are not turned by cranks.

(5)   The ignorant always seem so certain and the intelligent so uncertain.

(6)   It's much easier to make money than it is to make a living.

(7)   A desk is a wastebasket with drawers.

(8)   The other man's word is an opinion, yours is the truth, and your boss's is law.

Peter's Theorem:

Incompetence plus incompetence equals incompetence.

Johnson's Corollary to Heller's Law:

Nobody really knows what is going on anywhere within your organization.

☞ You Wouldn't Believe the Things People Say About Government

Wiker's Law:

>   Government expands to absorb revenue, and then some.

Baxter's First Law:

>   Government intervention in the free market always leads to a lower national standard of living.

Baxter's Second Law:

>   The adoption of fractional gold reserves in a currency system always leads to depreciation, to devaluation, to demonetization, and, ultimately, to complete destruction of that currency.

Baxter's Third Law:

>   In a free market, good money drives bad money out of circulation.

Robertson's Rule:

>   A diplomat is someone who can tell you to go to hell in such a way that you will look forward to the trip.

Last on the Politician's Hit Parade:

>   I'll never promise you a rose garden.

Kamin's First Law:

> All currencies will decrease in value and purchasing power over the long term, unless they are freely and fully convertible into gold and that gold is traded freely without restrictions of any kind.

Kamin's Second Law:

> Threat of capital controls accelerates marginal capital outflows.

Kamin's Third Law:

> Combined total taxation from all levels of government always increases (until the government is replaced by war or revolution).

Kamin's Fourth Law:

> Government inflation is always worse than statistics indicate; central bankers are biased toward inflation when the money unit is nonconvertible and without gold or silver backing.

Kamin's Fifth Law:

> Purchasing power of currency is always lost far more rapidly than it is ever regained. (Those who expect even fluctuations in both directions play a losing game).

Genthe's Law:

> Federal regulatory agencies are self-canceling.

Diogenes' First Dictrum:

> The more heavily a man is supposed to be taxed, the more power he has to escape being taxed.

Furst's Bureaucratic Byword:

> Massive expenditures obscure the evidence of bad judgments.

Glomm's Law:

> The strong take from the weak, the rich take from the poor, and the government takes from everyone.

Nowlan's Truism:

> An "acceptable level of unemployment" means that the government economist to whom it is acceptable still has a job.

Neville's Conclusion:

> There's no special reason; it's just government policy.

Jonathan Swift's Law:

> Laws are like cobwebs, which may catch small flies, but let wasps and hornets break through.

Gummidge's Law:

> The amount of expertise varies in inverse proportion to the number of statements understood by the general public.

Katz's Law:

> Men and nations will act rationally when all other possibilities have been exhausted.

Long's Axiom:

> An elephant is a mouse built to government specifications.

Lani's Principles of Economics:

> (1) Taxes are not levied for the benefit of the taxed.
> (2) One hundred dollars placed at 7 per cent interest compounded quarterly for two hundred years will increase to more than $100 million, by which time it will be worth nothing.
> (3) In God we trust; all others pay cash.

McNaughton's Rule:
> Any argument worth making within a bureaucracy must be capable of being expressed in a simple declarative sentence that will be obviously true once it is stated.

Dyer's Law:
> The smaller or less important the government publication, the higher the grade and salary of the editor.

Krueger's Law:
> A taxpayer is someone who doesn't have to take a civil service examination to work for the government.

Nolan's Observation:
> There is nothing so asinine that governments will not proclaim it as official doctrine.

Johnson's Laws of Bureaucratic Immobility:
> (1)   Never do anything for the first time.
> (2)   Pay is a function of time spent.
> (3)   Wait until others have given clearance.
> (4)   It is futile, so why try?
> (5)   Make only big mistakes.

☞ Cogent Comments by Some Ordinary People and Some Not So Ordinary

Witcoff's Truism:
> You know you're getting old when everything dries up or leaks.

Baker's Law:
> Misery no longer loves company; nowadays it insists on it.

Gibb's Law:
> Infinity is one lawyer waiting for another.

Horowitz's First Law of the Admiralty:
> A collision at sea can ruin your entire day.

Blomgren's Law:
> Reality is a hypothesis.

Nienberg's Law:
> Progress is made on alternate Fridays.

An Earthy Observation:
> Blessed are the inept for they shall inherit the skies.

Makar's Conclusion:
> If it were not for the weather and sex, 98 per cent of the people wouldn't have anything to talk about.

Renson's Law:

> The longer somebody has to wait for a thing, the better he
> expects it to be.

Fletcher's Flagrant Rumination:

> Efficiency is a highly developed form of laziness.

Benchley's Law of Distinction:

> There are two kinds of people in this world: those who be-
> lieve the world can be divided into two kinds of people, and
> those who don't.

Goda's Truism:

> By the time you get to the point where you can make ends
> meet, somebody moves the ends.

Margolin's Law:

> Behind every successful man is an ass.

Kent's Law:

> The length of a meeting is inversely proportional to the
> number of attendees without chairs.

Peter's Paradox:

> Employees in a hierarchy do not really object to incompe-
> tence in their colleagues.

Cannon's Cogent Comment:

> The leak in the roof is never in the same location as the drip.

Andrew's Deduction:

> Attila the Hun came from a broken home.

The Essentials for Happiness Rule:
> Something to do, someone to love, and something to hope for.

Rudin's Law:
> In a crisis that forces a choice to be made among alternative courses of action, most people will choose the worst one possible.

Ponemon's Provocation:
> If you don't know who's to blame, you are!

Johnny Carson's Definition of the Smallest Interval of Time Known to Man:
> Despite the fact that computer speeds are measured in nanoseconds and picoseconds—one billionth and one trillionth of a second, respectively—the smallest interval of time known to man is that which occurs in Manhattan between the traffic signal turning green and the taxi driver behind you blowing his horn.

Firestone's Law of Forecasting:
> Chicken Little only has to be right once.

Simpson's Sage Sample:
> You can't tell a book by its lover.

Perhac's Conclusions:
> (1)   It's always greener on the other pool table.
> (2)   Put a little money away every month and at the end of the year you'll be surprised how little you have.

Oliver Herford's Rule:
> A kiss is a procedure, cunningly devised, for the mutual stoppage of speech at a moment when words are superfluous.

Shaw's Substantive:

>To err is human, but when the eraser wears out before the pencil, you're carrying it too far.

Laden's Suggestion:

>The family that bathes together, stays together.

Wood's Hypothesis:

>All things come to him who orders hash.

Beach's Postulate:

>Winners tell funny stories; losers holler "Deal!"

Sobel's Law:

>There's no substitute for genuine lack of preparation.

The Hippocrates Application:

>Happiness is merely the remission of pain.

Napier's Rule:

>Truth is like a trolley car that, to operate, has to run in alternating directions.

Pavlov's Principle:

>When the bell rings, there had better be some supper.

Mark Twain's Dictum:

>Be virtuous and you will be eccentric.

Mencken's Law:

>There is always an easy solution to every human problem—neat, plausible, and wrong.

Madson's question:

>If you have to travel on a *Titanic,* why not go first class?

Professor French's Caution:

>   If someone offers to get you a date with a June graduate from Vassar, make certain to ask, "June of what year?"

Robert Louis Stevenson's Conclusion:

>   Man is a creature who lives not upon bread alone but principally by catchwords.

Mark Twain's Postulate:

>   A man who carries a cat by the tail learns something he can learn in no other way.

Lacopi's Law:

>   After food and sex, man's greatest drive is to tell the other fellow how to do his job.

Bob Hope's Quip:

>   There are no new jokes, but a joke is new if you have never heard it before.

Julius Caesar's First Law of Aerodynamics of Hurled Objects:

>   *Sic pilum iactum est.* (Literal translation: That's the way the spear is thrown. Free translation: How come I always get the shaft?)

Bula's Basic Laws:

>   (1)   Supersonic travel means that, although you still can't be in two places at once, at least you can be heard trying.
>   (2)   Noel Coward thought work was more fun than fun, but he never, ever, worked in the mines.
>   (3)   Time is money, as many merry widows have proved.
>   (4)   Inflation rates testify to the worldwide popularity of wishful thinking.

Gleason's Thought for the Day:

> Have a brother explain the reason for the "Odd Fellows" lodge.

Boyle's Truism:

> One who has a clear conscience has a foggy memory.

An Old Chestnut:

> There is no such thing as being a "little pregnant."

Wishful Thinking:

> Nostalgia isn't what it used to be.

Keenan's Truism:

> Gratitude is for favors to come.

Diogenes' Second Dictum:

> If a taxpayer thinks he can cheat safely, he probably will.

Craig's Rule:

> Genius starts at the top and works up.

Q's Law:

> No matter what stage of completion one reaches in a North Sea oil project, the cost of the remainder of the project remains the same.

Matsch's Law:

> It is better to have a horrible ending than to have horrors without end.

Farber's Laws:

> (1)   Give him an inch and he'll screw you.
> (2)   We're all going down the same road in different directions.

(3) Necessity is the mother of strange bedfellows.

(4) You have taken yourself too seriously.

Benjamin Disraeli's Maxim:
"Frank and explicit"—that is the right line to take when you wish to conceal your own mind and confuse the mind of others.

Murphy's Metric Recommendation:
We should go metric every inch of the way.

Murphy's Design Maxim:
Either the box is too small and won't work, or it's too·big and won't fit.

The Shrink's Opinion of Murphy:
Down deep, Murphy is shallow.

Howard's Homily:
Every time you learn all the answers, they change all the questions.

Lanham's Law:
The first Christian gets the hungriest lion.

Murphy's Twelfth Law:
You can't lead a cavalry charge if you think you look funny on a horse.

Wingfield's Probability:
Accuracy is the sum total of your compensating mistakes.

Weinberg's Observation:
The pot at the end of the rainbow is not Acapulco Gold.

Millard's Conclusions:

(1)   The universe is simple; it's the explanation that's complex.

(2)   Television is to media what hydrogen bombs are to explosives.

(3)   You don't have to fool all the people all the time—just the right people part of the time.

(4)   There is no such thing as a motiveless crime.

Fuller's Rule:

He who laughs last has no sense of humor.

Millie's Maxim:

Nothing is quite so annoying as to have someone go right on talking when you're interrupting.

Arthur Litoff's Truism:

Before the marriage, women's glib; after the marriage, Women's Lib.

Kelch's Observation:

Beauty is only skin deep, but ugly goes all the way to the bone.

Clark's Law:

A new roll of toilet tissue is never installed by the person using the last of the previous roll.

Hylton's Rule:

No job is too small to botch.

Thoreau's Law:

If you see someone approaching with the obvious intent of doing you good, run for your life.

Mrs. Jacobsen's Rumination:
>   Apple pie without the cheese is like a kiss without a squeeze.

Gregory's Lament:
>   Philosophically, I quest perfection; physically, I procrastinate.

Map Librarian's Postulate:
>   Philadelphia is a nice place to live, but you wouldn't want to visit there.

Librarian's Motto:
>   Information is where you find it.

Mark Twain's Observation:
>   Sometimes too much to drink is barely enough.

Wagner's Law:
>   The joy of contemplating another's misfortunes is the purest of joy.

Rombauer's Rigid Rule:
>   A watched pot never boils—unless you light the gas under it.

Dean Martin's Definition of Drunkenness:
>   You're not drunk if you can lie on the floor without holding on.

Saunders' Saying:
>   Society is less threatened by the fat around the middles than it is menaced by the fat between the ears.

Larrimer's Constant to the Improvement of Life:
>   What this world needs is a damned good plague.

Long's Notes:

>   (1)   The greatest productive force is human selfishness.
>
>   (2)   A skunk is better company than a person who prides themselves on being "frank."
>
>   (3)   Always listen to experts: they'll tell you what can't be done, and why; then do it.

Balzac's Rule:

>   The dimmer the light, the greater the scandal.

Van Roy's Axioms:

>   (1)   Help fight truth decay.
>
>   (2)   Love makes the world go round, but it's the lack of money that keeps it flat.

Sam Snead's Principle:

>   Never up—never win.

Launegayer's Maxim:

>   If at first you don't succeed—so much for skydiving.

Sam's Axioms:

>   (1)   Any line, however short, is still too long.
>
>   (2)   Work is the crab grass of life, but money is the water that keeps it green.

Hoffman's Law of Conservation:

>   Next to the dog, the wastebasket is man's best friend.

Steele's Plagiarism of Somebody's Philosophy:

>   Everyone should believe in something—I believe I'll have another drink.

Osborn's Law:

>   Variables won't; constants aren't.

Grandma Soderquist's Conclusion:

There are more horses' asses in this world than there are horses.

Freud's Law of Revoltin' Developments:

> After a relaxing night of sleep, tense up to meet the day.

Gordon's Insertion:

> A loud voice is a reasonable equivalent of a good eye.

Preston's Postulates:

(1)   The pen is mightier than the pencil.

(2)   I disagree with what you say, but I will defend to the death your right to tell such lies.

(3)   Chaste makes waste.

(4)   The devil finds work for idle glands.

(5)   A penny saved is ridiculous.

(6)   He who always finds fault with his friends has faulty friends.

(7)   Where there's a will, there's an inheritance tax.

(8)   Money is the root of all evil and man needs roots.

(9)   It's not the money, it's the principal and the interest.

(10)   Ask not for whom the bell tolls and you will pay only the station-to-station rate.

(11)   He who is flogged by fate and laughs the louder is a masochist.

Smyth's Summation:

> The facts, although interesting, are irrelevant.

B. V. Roy's Collection:

(1)   A nut easy to crack is often empty.

(2)   Every day the rest of the world gets nearer and dearer to us.

(3)   Sweet wine often turns a nice woman sour.

(4)   On the highway, beware of rolling stoned.

☞ Quotes for Offices, No Matter What the Business

Yamamoto's Translated Theorem of Behavior:
> Two longs don't make a light.

The "Make Your Own Breaks" Credo:
> Success is a matter of luck; just ask any failure.

Ross's Law:
> Never characterize the importance of a statement in advance.

Jenkinson's Law:
> It won't work.

Wynne's Law:
> Negative slack tends to increase.

Cohen's Corollary:
> A little money is good, but large sums foul the works.

Cunningham's Conclusion:
> Coincidence is common; it may be the rule.

The Savings-and-Loan Law:
> Save your money—someday it may be worth something.

Renau's Ramblings:

    (1)   Old fan dancers should wear orthopedic G strings.

    (2)   Crowded elevators smell different to midgets.

    (3)   Some bosses are fair to everyone—they're mean to everybody.

The "Oh, Forget It" Law:

    The best way to forget your own problems is to help someone else with theirs.

Pearson's Postulate:

    It requires a very unusual mind to make an analysis of the obvious.

Hubbard's Law:

    The world gets better every day—then worse again in the evening.

Levine's Axiom:

    We speak of unemployment as though work were a four-letter word.

Steiner's Statement:

    The careful application of terror is also a form of communication.

Bill's Note:

    A cluttered desk=a man of genius.

Richardson's Rule:

    Satisfaction is, in itself, success.

The Gossage Rule on Copywriting:

    Plagiarize, plagiarize, but call it research.

Maas's Maxim:
>A fool and his guilt are soon parted.

Captain Jack's Viewpoint:
>If you are good, you'll be assigned all the work. If you are really good, you'll get out of doing it.

Kovalevski's Dictum:
>If credit can possibly go to someone else, it will.

Galef's Laws:
>(1) If there are too many cooks—it's the union rules.
>(2) The early bird suffers from insomnia.

Observations of a Philosopher:
>(1) Nothing is opened more often by mistake than the mouth.
>(2) Years make us old—people make us wise.
>(3) A laugh is just a simple thimbleful in the infinite number of joys.
>(4) A meeting is no substitute for progress.

Spark's Law of Irrepressible Use:
>If a person has something, they feel compelled to use it even though its use is unnecessary. *Examples:* The child who gets a hammer uses it. The person who gets authority will overexercise it.

Robert Frost's Observation:
>A bank is a place where they lend you an umbrella in fair weather and ask for it back when it starts to rain.

Simenon's Profound Postulate:
>All proverbs contradict each other.

Van Roy's Rumination:
> Fools rush in where fools have been before.

MacKenzie's First Law:
> If it's not on paper, it doesn't exist.

Cole's Rules:
> (1)   The human mind is like a parachute—it functions best when it is open.
>
> (2)   The only angle from which to approach a problem is the try-angle.

The Ultimate Wisdom:
> The only alternative to perseverance is failure.

Maiorella's Mistake:
> You only think it is possible to exceed the limits of possibility.

Becker's Law:
> It's always much harder to find a job than to keep one.

Lord Falkland's Rule:
> When it is not necessary to make a decision, it is necessary not to make a decision.

Fitz-Gibbon's Law:
> Creativity varies inversely with the number of cooks involved with the broth.

Holoway's Hollering:
> It's better to be lucky than smart.

John Newbern's Law:

> People can be divided into three groups: those who make things happen, those who watch things happen, and those who wonder what happened.

Horner's Five-Thumb Postulate:

> Experience varies directly with equipment ruined.

Bukota's Typographical Truths:

> (1) Typographical errors will be found only after the final copy is bound and mailed.
>
> (2) Typographical errors appear in inverse proportion to the number of syllables in the misspelled word.
>
> (3) Engineers can catch misspellings only in words written by someone that's not an engineer.
>
> (4) The incidence of missed typographical errors increases in direct proportion to the number of people who will see the copy.
>
> (5) The incidence of missed typographical errors increases in direct proportion to the size of the letters in the copy (about 1.3 errors per point size, but that proportion isn't proven beyond doubt).
>
> (6) Success in finding typographical errors is in inverse proportion to the finder's income and number of years of education. Ask the janitor.

Murrow's Observation:

> The obscure we see eventually; the completely apparent takes longer.

Dr. Boyson's Rule:

> When policy fails, try thinking.

Hadley's Law:

> Don't ever confuse motion with progress.

Gordie's Thought:

> Only the stupid, the hurried, and the strong close a reference
> book upon satisfactory completion of the original search.

Kelso's Observation:

> The only one who got everything done by Friday was Robin-
> son Crusoe.

An Advertising Axiom:

> Early to bed, early to rise, work like hell, and advertise.

Pope's Rule:

> Blessed is he who expects nothing, for he shall never be dis-
> appointed.

The Transcription Law:

> The number of errors made is equal to the number of
> squares employed.

Field's First Law of Success:

> If at first you don't succeed, try, try again. Then quit. No
> use being a damn fool about it.

Zymurgy's Law on the Availability of Volunteer Labor:

> People are always available for work in the past tense.

Zymurgy's First Law of Evolving-System Dynamics:

> Once you open a can of worms, the only way to recan them
> is to use a longer can.

Sheetz's Ruminations:

> (1)   It's not whether you win or lose, but how you place
> the blame.
> (2)   A friend in need is a friend to avoid.

(3) You don't have to be a cannibal to get fed up with people.

(4) To err is human; to forgive is against company policy.

(5) When it comes to giving, some people stop at nothing.

(6) The way some people find fault, you'd think there was a reward.

(7) Those who think they know it all are very annoying to those who do.

Lewis' Lament:

When all is said and done, there's more said than done.

Mesikimen's Law:

There's never time to do it right, but always time to do it over.

Gianni's CPA Rule:

An assumption is the first step toward a screw-up.

Davidson's Law of Inquiry:

People ask stupid questions for a reason.

Robbin's Rules of Marketing:

(1) Your share of the market is really lower than you think.

(2) Never delay the end of a meeting or the beginning of a cocktail hour.

(3) The combined market position goals of all competitors always totals at least 150 per cent.

(4) The existence of a market does not insure the existence of a customer.

(5) Strategies develop most easily from big backlogs.

(6) Beware of alleged needs that have no real market.

(7) The worth of a thing is what it will bring.

(8)   Low price and long shipment will win over high price and short shipment.

(9)   Umbrella pricing encourages noncompetitive costs.

(10)   The competition really can have lower prices.

(11)   If you can't get the whole job, settle for part of it.

(12)   The number of competitors never declines.

(13)   Secret negotiations are usually neither.

(14)   A good presentation has as many questions as answers.

(15)   If the customer wants vanilla, give him vanilla.

(16)   If the customer buys lunch, you've lost the order.

(17)   Unless constantly nurtured, nothing is as short-lived as a good customer.

(18)   No matter how good the deal, the customer is always skeptical.

White's Observations of Committee Operation:

(1)   People very rarely think in groups; they talk together, they exchange information, they adjudicate, they make compromises. But they do not think; they do not create.

(2)   A really new idea affronts current agreement.

Dalgish's Law:

Good judgment comes from experience; experience comes from bad judgment.

Gill's Law:

Not a shred of evidence exists in favor of the idea that life is serious.

Rahilly's Rule for Secretarial Efficiency:

Work smarder and not harder and be careful or yor spelling.

Stovall's Law of Negative Inaction:

> The only thing wrong with doing nothing is that you never know when you're finished.

Allen's Truism:

> He who attacks must vanquish; he who defends must merely survive.

Thurber's Law:

> There is no safety in numbers, or anything else.

Ward's Laws:

> (1)   Those who live by their wits are obliged to live beyond their means.
>
> (2)   Neither snow, nor rain, nor heat, nor gloom of night slows mail arriving at its destination as effectively as the affixing of a special delivery stamp.

Stockmeyer's Theorem:

> If it looks easy, it's tough. If it looks tough, it's damn near impossible.

Gresham's Law:

> Trivial matters are handled promptly; important matters are never solved.

Couvier's Law:

> There's nothing more frightening than ignorance in action.

Rayburn's Rule:

> If you want to get along, go along.

archy's maxim:

> an optimist is a guy that has never had much experience

Yeck's Rumination:
> Luck is the chief factor behind the other fellow's success.

Bittel's Theory of Mass Dynamics:
> I'd be a pessimist, but it wouldn't work anyway.

The Law of Thumb:
> Somebody who thinks logically is a nice contrast to the real world.

Kostreski's Theory:
> If at first you don't succeed—find someone who knows what he's doing.

Martin-Berthelot's Principle:
> Of all possible committee reactions to any given agenda item, the action that will occur is the one which will liberate the greatest amount of hot air.

Ray's Rueful Rumination:
> The world is full of surprises, very few of which are pleasant.

Law of Selective Advancement:
> The man who knows "how" will always have a job. The man who knows "why" will always be his boss.

Linton's Laws:
> (1) Growth is directly proportionate to promises made; profit is inversely proportionate to promises kept.
> (2) An accurate determination of the depth of the well cannot be made by measuring the pump handle.
> (3) A picture is worth a thousand words; a slide show is both.

Cannon's Cogent Comment:
> If you tell the boss you were late for work because you had a flat tire, the next morning you will have a flat tire.

A Traveling Man's First Law:
> Nothing vouchered, nothing gained.

Captain Risser's Law:
> If it's in stock, we have it.

Gossage's Corollary:
> If you come up with a lemon, make lemonade.

Swinging-Door Maxim:
> Some say PUSH is the secret of success, others say PULL.

Drooker's Drool:
> No one can be unhappy while eating a bagel.

Podnos' Law:
> One is tolerant only of that which does not concern him.

The Law of Superiority:
> The first example of a superior principle is always inferior to the developed example of a inferior principle.

Lenz's Law:
> Experience is what you get when you didn't get what you wanted.

Hood's Warning:
> Be sure the brain is engaged before putting the mouth in gear.

Nolan's Observation:
> The difference between smart people and dumb people isn't that smart people don't make mistakes. They just don't keep making the same mistake over and over again.

Jack and Eric's Law:
> All work and no play means you make money hand over fist.

Comb's Truths of Management:
> (1)   To err is human; to forgive is not our policy.
>
> (2)   A good manager makes the correct decision on the basis of few or no facts.
>
> (3)   Never make a decision until the last possible moment; you may receive new information.

Cundall's Conclusion:
> Letters beginning "Dear Sir" will always be opened by a woman, usually an officer in the Women's Lib movement.

Cundall's Typing Theory:
> The amount of typing which comes due on any one day in an office is in direct correlation to the absentee record of the office typist.

Cundall's Advertising Agency Rule:
> Advertising agencies which win major national promotion awards invariably lose the account immediately thereafter.

Thoughts for the Day:
> (1)   Make someone happy today—mind your own business.
>
> (2)   A sandwich is an attempt to make both ends meat.
>
> (3)   Those who think they know it all upset those of us who do.

Greeniaus's Summations:
>   (1)   If you're pushing fifty, that's exercise enough.
>   (2)   To say nothing often reflects a fine command of the English language.
>   (3)   I'd give my right arm to be ambidextrous.

Hutchinson's "Old Faithful" Aphorism:
>   Things are more like they are now than they ever have been before.

Bye's First Law of Model Railroading:
>   Anytime you wish to demonstrate something, the number of faults is proportional to the number of viewers.

Mark Twain's Postulate:
>   Always do right. This will gratify some people, and astonish the rest.

Grunewald's Thought for the Day:
>   In order to take someone for a ride, you have to be ready to go for a ride.

W. C. Field's Observation:
>   Dogs are no good, because the sons of bitches (and they are, you know) wet on flowers.

Dino's Wisdom:

    An aptly thrown cup and saucer is cheaper than any other form of therapy.

Chisholm's Law of Human Interaction:

> Anytime things appear to be going better—you have over-looked something.

Daniel's Rule:

> A man who wants to read and write must let the grass grow long.

Another Old Chestnut:

> The only perfect science is hindsight.

Booth's Barhopping Observation:

> A bartender who nips or steals a little but is courteous, jovial, and happy toward customers is worth more on the payroll than a computer-regulated, cash-checking, efficient grouch who doesn't make off with a single ounce of booze.

Malorekian's Law:

> A body in motion pushed by a huge fear doubles in force.

Gentry's Motto:

> All some people expect in life is a fair advantage.

Rupp's Laws:

> (1) Any instrument that requires amplification probably should not be heard.
> (2) In decorating Christmas trees, you always need one more string of lights.

Bryson's Rule:

> We get so concerned with urgent, we never have time to deal with the important.

Lucy's Law:

> The alternative to getting old is depressing.

Beginner's-Luck Definition:
> Being born with a silver spoon in your mouth.

The First Law of Mathematics:
> The answer has to look right.

Schwab's Commentary on Travel:
> You can never really get away—you can only take yourself somewhere else.

Grandmother Blackburn's Mental Umbrella:
> Always be prepared for the worst. If it happens, you are ready for it. If it doesn't, you will be pleasantly surprised.

Sherman's Rule:
> Use your talents. The woods would be silent if only the birds sang that sing the best.

Karl Marx's Afterthought:
> The masses are the opium of religion.

Whitehead's Rule:
> Seek simplicity, and distrust it.

Gordon's Axiom:
> Cynicism is as parasitic as patriotism, but as long as man is a damned idiot, both are necessary.

An Oscar Wilde-ism:
> What is a cynic? A man who knows the price of everything, and the value of nothing.

Van Tree's Verity:
> To install is holy, to sell divine.

Ettorre's Observation:
    The other line moves faster.

J. B. S. Haldane's Law:

    . . . the universe is not only queerer than we suppose, but queerer than we *can* suppose.

Courtois's Rule:

    If people listened to themselves more often, they'd talk less.

Parkinson's Laws:

    (1)   Work expands to fill the time available for its completion; the thing to be done swells in perceived importance and complexity in a direct ratio with the time to be spent in its completion.

    (2)   Expenditures rise to meet income.

    (3)   If there is a way to delay an important decision, the good bureaucracy, public or private, will find it.

    (4)   The number of people in any working group tends to increase regardless of the amount of work to be done.

Dolan's Law:

    We do the right thing accidentally far more often than on purpose.

Daughter Schwab's Commentary on Being Witty:

    If you're so funny, why aren't you happy?

Richards' Reasoning:

    Don't believe in superstition; it brings bad luck.

Levinson's Observations:

    (1)   Don't be so broadminded that your brains fall out.

    (2)   There is no mistake in life beyond which all is down hill.

    (3)   A doppess is always dropping things, but a shlemiel picks up after him.

Bartig's Maxim:
>   The best way to break a habit is to drop it.

Nonfunctioning-Instruments Definition:
>   Your car stalls fifty miles out on a desert road and the gas
>   gauge still registers FULL.

The Machinist's Law of Diminishing Dimensions:
>   Grease is cheaper than steel.

George Santayana's Rumination:
>   Fanaticism consists in redoubling your efforts when you have
>   forgotten your aim.

Peckham's Law:
>   Beauty times brains equals a constant.

Dr. Conklin's Summations:
>   (1)   The girl who can't dance says the band is lousy.
>   (2)   You should be very careful with your pretenses, for
>   you are what you pretend to be.
>   (3)   When you wish for something, two things will happen.
>   One of them is that you don't get your wish. The other is
>   that you do.
>   (4)   Gentlemen's agreements can get very ungentlemanly.
>   (5)   Corollary: Verbal agreements lead to verbal disa-
>   greements.
>   (6)   Corollary: In an argument, it is a mistake to allow
>   your opponent to establish the definitions of the situations.

The "I Got Troubles" Law:
>   Temper is what gets most of us into trouble. Pride is what
>   keeps us there.

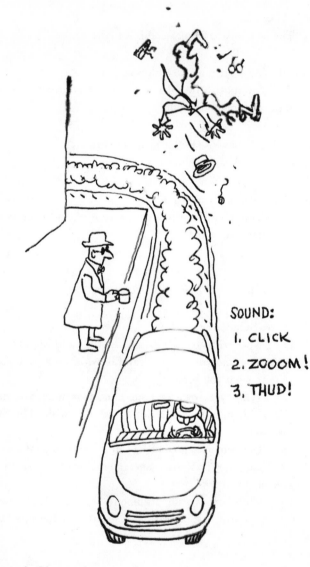

SOUND:
1. CLICK
2. ZOOOM!
3. THUD!

Brewer's Observation:
No good deed goes unpunished.

McFadden's Observation:

>It's true that money talks, but the only thing it says to some people is "Good-by."

McFadden's Addendum to *Poor Richard's Almanac:*

>To go to bed late and get up early, makes a man cross, mean, and surly.

Canada Bill Jones's Motto:

>It's morally wrong to allow suckers to keep their money.

The Second Theory of Relativity:

>If your parents didn't have children, odds are you won't either.

Satchel Paige's Law:

>Don't look back. Something might be gaining on you.

Nolan's Observation:

>Being free is no guarantee of happiness, but if you're unhappy, at least it will be on your own terms rather than someone else's.

The "It's the Only Way" Rule:

>Living well is the best revenge.

Zall's Law:

>(1)   Any time you get a mouthful of hot soup, the next thing you do will be wrong.
>(2)   How long a minute is, depends on which side of the bathroom door you're on.

Reeves's Old Russian Proverb:

>When you say "No," you never regret it.

Steiner's Statements:

(1)   Never eat in a restaurant named Mom's, play poker with a man named Doc, or buy a car from a man named Frenchy.

(2)   There's a great difference between right and wrong, but sometimes it's difficult to tell which is which.

(3)   Everything should be made as simple as possible, but no simpler.

The Digger's Dilemma, or the Law of Augmented Returns:

More dirt comes out of a hole than you can get back into it.

Schalk's Law:

If you have to tell people you're famous—you aren't.

Frenza's Rule:

A thing not looked for is seldom found.

Burr's Law:

You can fool some of the people all of the time and all of the people some of the time, and that's sufficient.

Smart's Rule:

When you tell a thing three times—it's true.

Sultan's Slant:

When no one is willing to listen to you, THINK.

John's Axiom:

When your opponent is down, kick him.

Van Roy's Law:

Buy in haste—repair at leisure.

Nowlan's Observation:

Ideally, every morning a man should be older, heavier, uglier, and have a deeper voice than his wife.

Canada Bill Jones's Supplement:
   A Smith & Wesson beats four aces.

Teller's Commentary:
> Whoever learns to control the weather will have destroyed the last safe topic of conversation.

Sam's Despair:
> The worst thing about ignorance is its insistency.

Sam's Sadness:
> Whatever goes up will go up some more after the first of the year.

Hartley's Second Law:
> Never sleep with anyone crazier than yourself.

George Bernard Shaw's Word:
> The lack of money is the root of all evil.

Subby's Simile:
> One man's meat is another man's poison, or, kitty heaven is mousie hell.

Weiler's Law:
> Nothing is impossible for the person who doesn't have to do it himself.

Mattuck's Directive:
> It's a law. Don't ask why—memorize it.

Seltzer's Suggestions:
> (1) If you don't want to see trees, stay out of the forest.
> (2) Do unto others as they should do unto you but won't.
> (3) It's the best of all possible worlds, and that's the way the ball bounces.

Simon's Law:
>   Everything put together sooner or later falls apart.

Judith Cohen's Assumption:
>   William Tell, Jr., had headaches.

Cook's Profound Principle:
>   A marksman is one who shoots first, and whatever he hits, he calls the target.

Goodman's Observations:
>   (1)   You promote creative thinking by reducing the number of subjects taught.
>   (2)   Technology is a way of multiplying the need for the unessential.

Bert's Bulwark:
>   If it is worth fighting for, it is worth fighting dirty for.

Fetridge's Law:
>   Important things that are supposed to happen do not happen, especially when people are looking.

Grandma Soderquist's Frustration:
>   Whenever Grandma bakes an apple pie, it's never, ever, quite up to Grandpa's mother's standards.

The Porcine Probability Principle:
>   Even a blind pig will find an acorn once in a while.

Ben Franklin's Observations:
>   (1)   Fish and guests smell in three days.
>   (2)   Tart words make no friends: a spoonful of honey will catch more flies than a gallon of vinegar.

(3)   Most people return small favors, acknowledge medium ones, and repay great ones—with ingratitude.

(4)   One rotten apple spoils the barrel.

(5)   Love your neighbor, but don't tear down your hedges.

(6)   Love your enemies, for they will tell you your faults.

(7)   Whoever lies with dogs, rises with fleas.

(8)   In the affairs of the world, men are saved not by faith but by the lack of it.

Law of Despair:
>   You can't thrust your hands deeply into your pockets if the holes in them are too large.

Napier's Maxim:
>   When you have a bottle of champagne, you will have something to celebrate.

First Law of Bridge:
>   It's always your partner's fault.

Kemper's Conclusion:
>   Everyone serves a purpose in life, even if it is to be a horrible example.

Allen's Principle:
>   The advantage of being a pessimist is that all your surprises are pleasant.

Loren William's Belief:
>   Objectivity is in the eye of the beholder.

The Fair-Weather-Friend Definition:
>   Those that borrow your lawn mower instead of your umbrella.

Cliff's Law:
> Never stand between a dog and the hydrant.

Knight's Notion:
> Curiosity kills more mice than cats.

Leach's Observation:
> Don't knock irritants. How else would we get pearls?

Poor's Law of Game Theory:
> Most games are easier to kibitz than to play.

Professor Gordon's Rule of Evolving Bryographic Systems:
> While bryographic plants are typically encountered in substrata of earthy or mineral matter in concreted state, discrete substrata elements occasionally display a roughly spherical configuration which, in the presence of suitable gravitational and other effects, lends itself to combine translatory and rotational motion. One notices in such cases an absence of the otherwise typical accretion of bryophyta. We therefore conclude that a rolling stone gathers no moss.

Vali's Axiom:
> In any human enterprise, works seeks the lowest hierarchical level.

Telly's Truisms:
> (1)   A sinner can reform, but stupid is forever.
> (2)   One seventh of our lives is spent on Mondays.

Ornithologist's Theory:
> One good tern deserves another.

Marcus Aurelius' Maxim:
>   A man's life is dyed the color of his imagination.

Martha's Maxim:
>   If you cast your bread upon the waters, it will return soggy.

Hill's First Law of Salesmanship:
>   Treat the customer like a mushroom; keep him in the dark and spread manure on him at frequent intervals.

Glatter's Rule:
>   Always eat before going to a wedding, funeral, confirmation, or bar mitzvah because it will be a long time between services and meals.

Bucy's Law:
>   Nothing is ever accomplished by a reasonable man.

Schafer's Axiom:
>   Children, as a class, flunk.

The Ultimate-Confusion Rule:
>   The little boy who dropped his chewing gum in the chicken yard.

Jones's Law:
>   The man who can smile when things go wrong has thought of someone he can blame it on.

Jones's Motto:
>   Friends may come and go, but enemies accumulate.

McClaughry's Codicil on Jones's Motto:
>   To make an enemy, do someone a favor.

The First Law of Debate:
>   Never argue with a fool—people might not know the difference.

Van Hoffman's Adage:
>   We are the people our parents warned us against.

Cusick's Postulate:
>   Suicide is confession and confession is suicide.

The Law of Probable Dispersal, or the "How Come it All Landed on Me?" Law:
>   Whatever hits the fan will not be evenly distributed.

Sociology's Iron Law of Oligarchy:
>   In every organized activity, no matter the sphere, a small number will become the oligarchical leaders and the others will follow.

Horace's Hypothesis:
>   Life is largely a matter of expectation.

Pastore's Truths:
>   (1)   Even paranoids have enemies.
>   (2)   This job is marginally better than daytime TV.
>   (3)   Regarding alcohol, four is more than more than enough.

Green's Law:

> You cannot afford to be funny unless you are paid for it.

Pudder's Law:

> Anything that begins well ends badly. Anything that begins badly ends worse.

George's Lament:

> The one exception to the rule that what goes up must come down is the landing gear.

Lowery's Law:

> If it jams, force it. If it breaks, it needed replacing anyway.

Starr's Law:

> It's only the people who you don't know who know what they're doing.

Gentry's Rule:

> If ambition doesn't hurt, you haven't got it.

Ferris' Frothing:

> Whatever their faults, the Communists never created canned laughter.

Kelly's Observations:

> (1) Living in the past has one thing in its favor—it's cheaper.
> (2) Lots of people suffer from saloon arthritis—every night they get stiff in another joint.

Mom's Law:

> If you play with anything long enough, it breaks.

Searle's Sage Sample:

The cussedness of inanimate objects is beyond understanding.

Raven's Ravings:

   (1)   *"Gesundheit"* means "shut up" in English.

   (2)   The way to a man's heart is through his veins.

   (3)   An energy crisis will never stop motor-mouths.

   (4)   The best things in life aren't things.

   (5)   If at first you don't succeed, clutch for whatever you can get.

Flucard's Corollary:

   Anything dropped in the bathroom falls in the toilet.

Wright's Conclusion:

   Man cannot live by broad alone.

Mahr's Law of Restrained Involvement:

   Don't get any on you.

Dad's Longevity Law:

   Abstain from wine, women, and song. Mostly song.

The Go-Getter Rule:

   Let them that don't want none have memories of not gettin' any.

Parkinson's Law of Delay:

   Delay is the deadliest form of denial.

The Apothegm of Disillusioned Wisdom:

   The only way to compensate for the shortness of life is to wear a long face.

Mark Twain's Law of Fisticuffs:

   Place your nose firmly between your opponent's teeth and throw him heavily to the ground on top of you.

Ellenberg's Theory:
>   One good turn gets most of the blanket.

The Tarnished Golden Rule:
>   (1)   Do unto others and do it fast.
>   (2)   Do unto others before they do unto you.

Cannon's Cogent Comments:
>   (1)   You are not a carpenter until you've run one finger through the saw; if you run too many fingers through the saw, you're not a carpenter.
>   (2)   A fool and his money share the same mattress.

Milton Friedman's Observation:
>   Human beings are distinguished from other animals more by their ability to rationalize than their ability to reason.

The Happy Hunter's Prayer:
>   Let me meet a girl who already has had enough to drink.

Ziegler's Observation:
>   It's a great life, if you weaken early enough to enjoy it.

The Attorney's Axiom:
>   Every good question breeds good and bad questions—and usually the person who asks the bad questions can't be stopped by good answers.

Dr. August's Law:
>   The less influence you have—the longer you wait.

Winston Churchill's Commentary on Man:
>   Man will occasionally stumble over the truth, but most of the time he just picks himself up and stumbles on.

Babe Ruth's Rule:
> Him what hits 'em goes and gits 'em.

Bonetti's Law:
> The less you bet, the more you lose when you win.

Porter's Axiom:
> Pain is forgotten; insult lingers on.

Law of Selective Attractiveness:
> Getting anything changes it from being desirable to just being taken for granted.

Martino's Corollary:
> It's not what you don't know that hurts you; it's all those things you know that aren't so.

Ponsy's Postulates:
> (1) Pray as if it were up to God, but work as if it were up to you.
> (2) He who blows his horn the loudest, does so because he's usually in a fog.
> (3) A speech, to be immortal, does not have to be eternal.
> (4) Intuition is reason in a hurry.
> (5) Behind every successful man, is a surprised mother-in-law.
> (6) Many a person has gone to their sarcophagus by what they put down their esophagus.

Bohor's Bromide:
> Old age and treachery will overcome youth and skill.

Plaut's Postulate:
> Apathy is becoming a major problem—but who cares?

The Undertaker's Amendment:
> Every shroud has a silver lining.

The Sukhomlinov Law:
> The most brilliantly dressed army will usually lose.

Max's Maxim:
> I'm for whoever gets you through the night—whether he be Jesus Christ or Jack Daniel.

Hagerty's Law:
> If you lose your temper at a newspaper columnist, he'll get rich or famous or both.

The Apartment Dweller's Law:
> Your upstairs neighbors dance, your downstairs neighbors hit the roof, and your next-door neighbors play handball.

The Apartment Dweller's Corollary:
> Neighbors never sleep.

Busch's Logical Conclusion:
> When you are young, your security is your youth. When you are old, you damn well better have money.

Sid's Sayings:
> (1) You can't win them all, if you don't win the first one.
> (2) You never learn anything with your mouth open.

Buerk's Conclusion:
> (1) Always know where the exit is.
> (2) Anticipate trouble, but don't go out looking for it.
> (3) Assume nothing.
> (4) All behavior is purposeful.

Schwartz's Observation:

Just because you're paranoid doesn't mean you're not being followed.

More of Murphy's Laws:

(1)   "In closing" is always followed by the other half of the speech.

(2)   Old boomerangs are hard to throw away.

(3)   The whole world is on back order.

(4)   All things are possible except skiing through a revolving door.

(5)   Hell has no fury like an unjustified assumption.

Mottler's Conclusion:

The scheduled program that is most widely publicized locally will be pre-empted nationally.

Lazarus' Observation:

Familiarity breeds consent.

Hoffman's Corollary:

The number of times you "gotta go" has a direct correlation with the number of toilets in the house.

Ferris' Conclusion:

Middle age is that wonderful period between the time when you don't know how and the time when you can't.

Ferris' Question:

It may be nature's way for mules to bray and chickens to cackle, but why must they always congregate in TV's studio audiences?

Keegan's Corollary:

Many Irishmen grow grapes—for raisins of their own.

Grandma Soderquist's Sage Thought:

The family that has taffy-pulls together, sticks together.

Golden Rules of Indulgence:
    (1)   Everything in excess.
    (2)   To enjoy the full flavor of life, always take big bites.
    (3)   Moderation is for monks.

McGoon's Law:
    The probability of winning is inversely proportional to the amount of the wager.

Gumperson's Laws of Perverse Opposites:
    (1)   The forecasting record of the Weather Bureau, despite its use of the most advanced equipment, technology and highly trained personnel, was not as good as that of *The Old Farmer's Almanac*.
    (2)   The girl at the race track who bets according to the color of the jockeys' shirts picks more winners than the man who has studied the past performance of every horse on the program.
    (3)   After a raise in salary you will have less money at the end of the month than you had before.
    (4)   The person who buys the most raffle tickets has the least chance of winning.

Shafer's Truisms:
    SUPPLY AND DEMAND: Lack of money is the root of all compromise.

    THE NUCLEAR REACTOR HYPOTHESIS: We'll all go together when we go.

    THE SECURITY OATH: Ask your mother.

    THE DISILLUSIONMENT PRINCIPLE: There's nothing new under the sun.

    THE BUDDY SYSTEM: Succeed on your own, or not at all.

THE DIPLOMACY PLOY: If you don't grow vegetables, it helps to praise and admire the garden in your neighbor's yard.

THE "PAY-OFF" THEORY: Only losers believe in luck, horses, horoscopes, and lotteries.

PROGRESS METHODOLOGY: Bribes and threats produce miracles.

THE ULTIMATE ONE-UPMANSHIP: Be sure your dog can lick every dog in your neighborhood.

THE BEHAVIOR-MODIFICATION CONCEPT: Some people are born rich and some are born poor. Rich is better.

THE FUTURE-SHOCK HYPOTHESIS: The time to leave is when the tar is hot, the feathers loose, and you see two men walking toward you with a pole.

THE EMPLOYEE'S POSITION: The establishment in any field seldom earns it pay.

THE "WE DO IT ALL FOR YOU" FUNCTION: The function of McDonald's is quite simple: Women's Liberation.

THE AMERICAN INDIAN CONCLUSION: When the chips are down, guns and troops count more than beads and blankets.

Meade's Maxim:
> Always remember that you are absolutely unique. Just like everyone else.

Telly's Truism:
> Not all heads are perfect—some have hair on them.

The Airplane Law:
> When the plane you are on is late, the plane you want to transfer to is on time.

The Law of the Lost Inch:
> In designing any type of construction, no over-all dimension can be correctly totaled after 4 P.M. Friday.
> Corollary 1: Under the same conditions, if any minor dimensions are given to $\frac{1}{16}$th of an inch, they cannot be totaled at all.
> Corollary 2: The correct total will be self-evident at 9:01 Monday morning.

Shalit's Law:
> The intensity of movie publicity is in inverse ratio to the quality of the movie.

The Antique Dealer's Law:
> If you've seen one artifact—you've seen them all.

Quaiver's Law:

 Most convicted criminals appeal to judges.

A Historical Possibility:

 Bluebeard collected alimony.

Greene's Rule:

 The best thing to hold onto in this world is each other.

Keith's Observation:

 The squeaky wheel doesn't always get greased; it often gets replaced.

Tarne's Truism:

 For youth, the length of a summer evening is inversely proportionate to the number of children playing in the block.

Bell's Rumination:

 Nothing stimulates the appetite like an empty billfold.

Stanley Marcus' Postulate:

 When business is good, no buyer is ever as good as she thinks she is; when business is bad, no buyer is ever as bad as management thinks she is.

Ruzek's Laws:

 (1) Humor is serious business.
 (2) People are promoted not by what they can do, but what people think they can do.

Chisholm's Second Law:

 Proposals, as understood by the proposer, will be judged otherwise by others.
 Corollary 1: If you explain so clearly that nobody can misunderstand, somebody will.

Corollary 2: If you do something which you are sure will meet with everyone's approval, somebody won't like it.

Corollary 3: Procedures devised to implement the purpose won't quite work.

Corollary 4: No matter how long or how many times you explain, no one is listening.

Van Oech's Law:

An expert really doesn't know anymore than you do. He is merely better organized and has slides.

Harding's Happy Homily:

It's hard to be nostalgic when you can't remember anything.

Malek's Law:

Any simple idea will be worded in the most complicated way.

Henry the Movie-Goer's Rule:

You have to stay to the end of the movie to find out how it comes out.

T. H. White's Conclusion:

The most difficult thing in the world is to know how to do a thing and to watch someone else doing it wrong, without commenting.

George Bernard Shaw's Principle:

Build a system that even a fool can use, and only a fool will want to use it.

The "Don't Look Behind You" Axiom:

The past was employed, but didn't work.

Beifeld's Principle:

The probability of a young man meeting a desirable and receptive young female increases by pyramidal progression when he is already in the company of (1) a date, (2) his wife, and (3) a better-looking and richer male friend.

Longfellow's Observation:

It takes less time to do something right than it takes to explain why you did it wrong.

Griffin's Law:

To live forever, acquire a chronic illness and take care of it.

Kipling's Errata:

If you keep your head when all about you are losing theirs, you don't understand the problem.

William's Law:

There is no mechanical problem so difficult that it cannot be solved by brute strength and ignorance.

Ben Franklin's Basic Law of Confidentiality:

Three may keep a secret, if two of them are dead.

Weaver's Law:

When several reporters share a cab on assignment, the reporter in the front seat always gets stuck for the fare.

Weaver's Corollary:

No matter how many reporters share a cab and no matter who pays, each puts the full fare on his own expense account.

Nostalgic Rumination No. 1:
> Pollution is increasing; remember when walking on water was a divine act?

Nostalgic Rumination No. 2:
> Remember when the word "plant" referred to a flower?

Anthony's Ruminations:
> (1) Little white lies are for golfers.
> (2) πr^2 is a Grecian formula.
> (3) Equal opportunities are for the dead.
> (4) Build a better mousetrap—if you hate cats.
> (5) Overpopulation is not a disease—it's a growth.

Van Roy's Postulates:
> (1) Never whisper to the deaf or wink at the blind.
> (2) You can't tell a book by its movie.
> (3) Recipe for trouble: believe all you hear and repeat it.

Paulsen's Rule:
> Enter a purported contest and be on the sponsor's sucker list for life.

Grandma Soderquist's Study of Human Nature:
> It'll save you an awful lot of time if, before entering any contest, you get a look at the judges.

The Law of Communications:
> The inevitable result of improved and enlarged communications between different levels of hierarchy is a vastly increased area of misunderstanding.

Lazar's Law:
> When in the course of human affairs—your spouse always finds out.

John's Law of Collateral:
    In order to get a loan, you must first prove you don't need it.

Raynes's Realistic Conclusion:
> A cynic is an idealist turned inside out.

Kitman's Law:
> Pure drivel on the TV screen tends to drive off ordinary drivel.

The "I Owe It All to My Better Half" Law:
> I am today, what my wife has made me. I shudder in fear when I think that maybe she'll change her mind again.

Kaufman's Rule:
> Agnosticism is legalistic religion.

The *Harper's Magazine* Law:
> You never find an article until you replace it.

A Rumination for Bachelors:
> A bachelor is a fox longing for the grapes he judges sour.

Johnson's Law:
> There's nothing to scratch but the surface.

Schiffman's Supplement:
> If you feed them well enough, they'll never remember what you said.

Vigue's Law:
> A man without a religion is like a fish without a bicycle.

Mrs. Murphy's Corollary or the Law of the Perversity of Nature:
> You cannot successfully determine beforehand which side of the bread to butter.

Gonzales' Observation:
> The passage of time is as amusing as a week-old burrito.

The Axiom of the Pipe:

> A pipe gives a wise man time to think and a fool something to stick in his mouth.

Roxalana's Rule:

> Just expect people to be people.

Flannegan's Finagling Factor:

> That quantity which, when multiplied by, divided by, added to, or subtracted from the answer you get, gives you the answer you should have gotten.

Martha's Maxim:

> If God had meant for us to travel tourist class, He would have made us narrower.

Dolores' Dabblings:

> (1) Promises are like babies: fun to make, but hell to deliver.
>
> (2) Infants speak many languages before they find one that grown-ups understand.
>
> (3) The amount of sleep needed by the average person is ten minutes more.

Chopin's Postulate:

> English is merely French spelled poorly, or all philosophies are different roads leading to the same station.

Booker's Law:

> An ounce of application is worth a ton of abstraction.

Brown's Law of Business Success:

> Our customer's paper work is profit. Our own paper work is loss.

Oler's Theorem:

>Everybody needs a certain level of misery in his life to ever be happy.

>Corollary 1: If his misery falls below his critical level, he becomes unhappy and is driven to seek new misery.

>Corollary 2: When his total misery rises to his critical level, he becomes happy again.

Suster's Rule:
>He who is most concerned is always last to hear.

Humpty Dumpty's Rumination:
>When I use a word, it means just what I choose it to mean —neither more nor less.

Alice's Corollary:
>The question is whether you *can* make words mean so many different things.

Lippka's Law:
>When the world falls into complete moral decay, don't be so old you can't enjoy it.

The Holiday Turkey Laws:
>(1)   The size of a turkey bears no relation to the amount of hash it will produce.
>
>(2)   At any given dinner where a single turkey is carved, three of the guests will ask for wings.
>
>(3)   Regardless of what time a wife serves a holiday dinner, it will cause her husband to miss the last half of the TV football game.
>
>(4)   The job of carving a turkey is always assigned to the person least capable of carrying it out.
>
>(5)   The space available in an electric refrigerator contracts or expands in inverse ratio to the amount of leftovers.

Samuel's Maxim:
>If you think the world is against you—it doesn't necessarily mean that it isn't.

Elkin's Law:
>If it's tainted money—it's usually because 'taint mine.

A Law of Changing Times:

>   Florists now go to school for a year to learn how to make real flowers look like plastic.

Whidden's Growl:

>   The amateur is the one with all the answers.

May's Mordant Maxim:

>   A university is a place where men of principle outnumber men of honor.

Cook's Cogitations:

>   (1) When putting cheese in a mousetrap, always leave room for the mouse.
>   (2) A little lie sometimes saves a ton of explanations.
>   (3) A theory is always better than its explanation.

Metcalfe's Musing:

>   Suicide is the sincerest form of self-criticism.

Big George's Observation:

>   The beauty of most women is inversely proportional to the distance of the observer.

Bula's Truisms:

>   (1) Beauty is only skin deep, but it's a superficial world.
>   (2) Beauty's in the eye of the beholder, yet pin-ups find plenty of room.

Schwartz's Law of Mathematics:

>   When in doubt, figure it out.

The Born-Loser Definition:

>   The guy who loses even in his own fantasies.

The Rule of Elderly Survival:

    If you are wearing one brown shoe and one black shoe, you
have a pair like it somewhere in the closet.

Clifton's Rules:

(1) Some people are like blisters—they never appear until the work is done.

(2) A poet can survive anything but a misprint.

(3) Some people will believe anything if it's whispered to them.

(4) Money no longer talks—it just goes without saying.

(5) Before borrowing money from a friend, decide which you need more.

(6) He who thinks he has no faults—has one.

Brandstadt's Observations:

(1) Boys will be boisterous.

(2) It pays to get drunk with the best people.

Beatt's Ruminations:

(1) Ours is the age which is proud of machines that think and suspicious of men who try to.

(2) The only people who know what's good for you are those who know what's good for them.

(3) Society is always taken by surprise at any new example of common sense.

(4) The praise of laymen is a habit-forming drug.

(5) Exchange of money is a zero-sum game; exchange of love is not.

The Cynic's Reflection:

I'd be a pessimist, but it wouldn't work anyway.

Kiddie's Constant:

There are coexisting elements in frustration phenomena which separate expected results from achieved results.

Doelger's Thought:

Among the uncertainties even a clouded crystal ball is of value.

☞ Inserts to Make a Speech Successful

Forfar's Fact:
> When you are right, no one remembers. When you are wrong, no one forgets.

Gilbert's Conclusion:
> People who park on the east side of a football stadium will invariably have seats on the west side.

Musial's Law:
> The driver's side windshield wiper always streaks and wears out first.

The Apartment Washing-Machine Corollary:
> Whenever you need to use the washer and drier, someone else will have beaten you to it, and, conversely, it's never in use when you don't need it.

Downs's Deduction:
> Family reunions are all relative.

Samuel's Sagacity:
> A cosigner is the man in the next cell.

The "Nature Abhors the Vertical" Law:
> Never stand when you can sit; never sit when you can lie down.

Simmon's Law:
>   The desire for racial integration increases with the square of
>   the distance from the actual event.

Sir George Savile's Rule:
>   Those who think money will do everything may well be sus-
>   pected of doing everything for money.

DeVyver's Law:
>   Given a sufficient number of people and an adequate
>   amount of time, you can create insurmountable opposition to
>   the most inconsequential idea.

Gerken's First Observation:
>   Mirrors are twice as good as windows—you only have to
>   clean one side to see clearly.

Gerken's Second Observation:
>   How can you tell if somebody's trying if they never succeed?

The Housewife's Lament:
>   Keeping house is like stringing beads with no knot in the end
>   of the thread.

The Spare-Parts Principle:
>   Accessibility during recovery of small parts which fall from
>   the work bench varies directly with the size of the part and
>   inversely with its importance to the completion of work un-
>   derway.

Anthony's Law of Force:
>   Don't force it; get a larger hammer.

Anthony's Law of the Workshop:

> Any tool, when dropped, will roll into the least accessible corner.

The Corollary to Anthony's Law of the Workshop:

> On its way to the corner, any dropped tool will always first strike your toes.

Pickett's Postulate:

> The person who snores the loudest will fall asleep first.

Hind's Hindsights:

> (1) Man is planned obsolescence.
>
> (2) If one keeps his socks clean and runs around with the right people—things fall into place.
>
> (3) We regret more things we didn't do than things we did do.

Magary's Law:

> In the summer, bus windows never open. In the winter, bus windows never close.

Goldsmith's Law:

> No shoelace ever broke being untied.

Terman's Law of Innovation:

> If you want a track team to win the high jump, you find one person who can jump seven feet, not seven people who can jump one foot.

The Borgia Family Byword:

> It is better to be hated than to be ignored.

Bill's Pill for All Ills:

> Although living to a ripe old age may not guarantee health, wealth, and happiness, it certainly beats the other alternative.

Dr. Conklin's Rules:

> (1) Having a second after-dinner drink is proof that you've had too many before-dinner drinks.
>
> (2) When it comes to corruption, nothing succeeds like money.
>
> (3) It is impossible to overdo luxury

Weinberg's Corollary:

> An expert is a person who avoids the small errors while sweeping on the grand fallacy.

The "Hi, Mom" Rule:

> Mothers-in-law are just like mothers, except you don't love them.

Creamer's Conclusion:

> When a man's wife learns to understand him, she usually stops listening to him.

Russ the Male Chauvinist's Observation:

> Even if you understood women, you'd never believe it.

The Bicycle Law:

> Thirty-pound bicycles need a twenty-pound lock and chain.
> Forty-pound bicycles need a ten-pound lock and chain.
> Fifty-pound bicycles need no lock and chain.

Sandra Litoff's First Rule on Husbands:
> The only thing worse than a husband who never notices what you cook or what you wear is a husband who always notices what you cook and what you wear.

The Light-Under-the-Bushel-Basket Law:
> Never do card tricks for the group you play poker with.

Don Kaul's Conclusion:
> Someday birds will fly the ocean like men—in big silver planes.

Mim's Messages:
> (1)   Eat, drink and be merry, for tomorrow you may diet.
> (2)   A word to the wicked: perfection ain't perfect.

The Carpenter's Rule:
> Cut to fit; beat into place.

The Show-Biz Axiom:
> The day before your singing debut, you will get laryngitis.

Gallagher's Insight:
> If spilled, there's no such thing as "a little water."

Howard's First Law of Theater:
> Use it.

Stamp's Traveler's Lament:
> Why is it that you arrive in Cedar Falls and your baggage arrives in Honolulu, but never the other way around?

Painter's Rule of the Road:

> Two wrongs won't make a right, but three rights will make a left.

Barker's Laws of the Highway:

> (1)   The only unoccupied toilet in the rest room is out of order.
>
> (2)   The service station will be out of toilet paper.
>
> (3)   The kids really have to go and you have to get the key to the rest room from the attendant—and he's busy.
>
> (4)   When you're in a hurry, the driver in the car in front of you will be pointing out the local points of interest to his passengers.
>
> (5)   The shortest distance between two points is under repair.

The Observation of Archimedes G. Bell:

> When a body is immersed in water—the telephone rings.

Zuliani's Law:

> An ill-dressed person may or may not be a bum, but a person who is always well dressed is surely a crook.

Defalque's Observations:

> (1)   Too many foreign countries are living beyond our means.
>
> (2)   A man's best friends are his ten fingers.
>
> (3)   Behind an able man there are always other able men.
>
> (4)   One should always play fair when he has the winning cards.
>
> (5)   Frequent naps will keep you from getting old— especially when taken while driving.
>
> (6)   Speak well of your enemies; remember you made them.

(7)   A man must do many good things to prove that he's good, but needs make only one mistake to prove that he's bad.

(8)   You cannot live on other people's promises, but if you promise others enough, you can live on your own.

Ross's Law:

Bare feet magnetize sharp objects so that they always point upward from the floor—especially in the dark.

Ginsburg's Law:

At the precise moment you take off your shoe in a shoestore, your big toe will pop out of your sock to see what's going on.

Petty's Poignant Philosophies:

(1)   If you want something badly, that's how you get it.

(2)   Many "get-rich-quick" schemes make millionaires— out of multi-millionaries.

Anderson's Law:

You can't depend on anyone to be wrong all the time.

Levy's Rumination:

Remarriage after divorce is the triumph of hope over experience.

Trusty Truism No. 23:

English started losing touch with reality with the word "if" and finished the job with the word "parameter."

The IRS Headache Law:

The wages of sin are unreported.

☞ Written Proof That Life Isn't All That Serious

Kegley's Principle of Deduction:
> If a pickpocket meets a saint, he sees only his pockets.

Kegley's Principle of Change:
> It is easier to behave your way into a new way of thinking than to think your way into a new way of behaving.

The Laws of Gardening:
> (1) Other people's tools work only in other people's yards.
> (2) Fancy gizmos don't work.
> (3) If nobody uses it, there's a reason.
> (4) You get the most of what you need the least.

Kelly's Postulate:
> A man is known by the company he keeps—avoiding.

Dr. Wood's Thought:
> It is better to have poor taste than no taste at all.

Red's Rumination:
> Even with a nightcap, a wolf looks nothing like a grandmother.

J. M. Barrie's Admission:

I am not young enough to know everything.

Levy's Laws:

(1) To have a sense of humor is to be a tragic figure.

(2) Any discovery is more likely to be exploited by the wicked than applied by the virtuous.

(3) No amount of genius can overcome a preoccupation with detail.

(4) Eternal boredom is the price of vigilance.

Gentry's Conclusion:

Virtue is just vice at rest.

James Abbott McNeill Whistler's Conclusion:

If other people are going to talk, conversation is simply impossible.

Johnson's Definition of Economics:

A study of how men make money and how women spend it.

Camp's Law:

A coup that is known in advance is a coup that does not take place.

Woolworth's Law:

Every crowd has a pilfer lining.

Johnson's Commentary on Incompatibility in Marriage:

I'm not incompatible—you're incompatible.

Lafferty's Law:

To test your capacity at a cocktail party, pinch both cheeks. If you feel nothing, have one more.

Nitzberg's Observations:

(1) A home is ruled by the sickest person in it.

(2) Some people have the personality of a STOP sign.

(3) If someone is terminally ill, he or she will usually stay alive for his or her birthday, anniversary, or some other special occasion.

Wolf's Law, or an Optimistic View of a Pessimistic World:
> It isn't that things will necessarily go wrong (Murphy's Law), but rather that they will take so much more time and effort than you think if they are *not* to go wrong.

Rice's Rumination:
> What the world needs is more geniuses with humility—there are so few of us left.

Henderson's Homily:
> The less you say, the less you have to take back.

Murphy's Thirteenth Law:
> There are no real secrets—only obfuscations.

Borstelmann's Rule:
> If everything seems to be coming your way, you're probably in the wrong lane.

Peter's Inversion:
> Internal consistency is valued more highly than efficiency.

Peter's Perfect-People Palliative:
> Each of us is a mixture of good qualities and some (perhaps) not-so-good qualities. In considering our fellow people, we should remember their good qualities and realize that their faults only prove that they are, after all, human. We should refrain from making harsh judgments of people just because they happen to be dirty, rotten, no-good sons-a-bitches.

Cohen's Laws of Innovation:
> (1)   Every innovative idea requires a finite number of dollars to convert it from concept to reality.

(2) After an initial threshold of financial support has been reached, the quality of the innovation is inversely proportional to the amount of money available for expenditures.

(3) Often the success of an innovative project is in the eyes of its creator.

Polly's Postulate:

Propinquity is a function of procreation.

Another of Robert's Rules:

Don't spend your gross salary.

Moise's Maxims:

(1) Eating a pound of fattening foods puts more weight on than not eating it takes off.

(2) The less chance you could successfully defend your income tax return, the greater the chance it will be randomly selected for audit.

Siwiak's Rule:

The only way to make something foolproof is to keep it away from fools.

Lyndon's Definition:

An optimist is a father who lets his teen-age son take the car on a date. A pessimist is a father who will not. A cynic is a father who did.

Strup's Law:

The importance of any given news event on television is directly proportionate to the amount of time remaining after the commercials.

The Phone Booth Rule:

A lone dime always gets the number nearly right.

The Lewis Law:

> If your outgo exceeds your income, your upkeep will be your downfall.

Mick's Musings:

> (1)   Unlike Will Rogers, I have met many men I did not like. Or even tolerate, for that matter.
>
> (2)   If you are so martyred as to sit still and let a bore blather on, you deserve your fate.
>
> (3)   No woman looks better in a fur coat than the animal who gave his life to provide it. Except Arthur Lipshitz, the animal who provided several for some of my more receptive friends. And he died with a smile on his face.
>
> (4)   If you cannot say something kind, don't say anything. Unless it is about my ex-husband, in which case cancel the above and let 'er rip.

Steinmetz's Rumination:

> There are no foolish questions, and no man becomes a fool until he stops asking questions.

Griffin's Thoughts:

> (1)   When you starve with a tiger, the tiger starves last.
>
> (2)   It's a wise man who lives with money in the bank. It's a fool who dies that way.

The Never-Lost-Hope Syndrome:

> It is always possible that someday 2 and 2 may turn out not to be four.

George Bernard Shaw's Reasoning:

> The reasonable man adapts himself to the world; the unreasonable one persists in trying to adapt the world to himself. Therefore all progress depends on the unreasonable man.

Long's Notes:

    (1)   A poet who reads his verse in public may have other nasty habits.

    (2)   It's better to copulate—than never.

    (3)   Don't try to have the last word; you might get it.

    (4)   Never appeal to a man's "better nature"—he might not have one.

    (5)   Secrecy is the beginning of tyranny.

    (6)   Be wary of strong drink. It can make you shoot at tax collectors and miss.

    (7)   Does history ever record any case in which the majority was right?

    (8)   You can go wrong by being too skeptical as readily as being too trusting.

    (9)   God is omnipotent, omniscient, and omnibenevolent. It says so right here on the label. If you have a mind capable of believing all three of these divine attributes simultaneously, I have a wonderful bargain for you. No checks, please. Cash, and in small bills.

The Fourteenth Corollary of Atwood's General Law of Dynamic Negatives:

    No books are lost by lending except those you particularly wanted to keep.

The Strategic Air Command Aircrew Theorem:

    The aircrews will win the war despite the plan from higher headquarters.

The Principle of the Modest Despot:

    All I want is the place next to mine.

The Rule of Accuracy:

>When working toward the solution of a problem, it always helps if you know the answer.

McClaughry's Law of Zoning:

>Where zoning is not needed, it will work perfectly; where it is desperately needed, it always breaks down.

O'Brien's $357.73 Theory:

>Auditors always reject any expense account with a bottom line divisible by 5 or 10.

Gumperson's Law:

>The probability of anything happening is in inverse ratio to its desirability.

An Old English Proverb:

>Dishonesty is never an accident. Good men, like good women, never see temptation when they meet it.

Form's Facts:

>(1) Peanut prizes inspire monkey contestants.
>(2) Poverty is life's cheapest lesson.

Norman Vincent Peale's Observation:

>America has become so tense and nervous it has been years since I've seen anyone asleep in church—and that's a bad situation.

Rear Admiral Pinney's Observations:

>(1) The closer one climbs to the top of the heap, the more clearly one sees the feet of clay.
>(2) If you don't get a reader's attention in the first paragraph, the remainder of your message is lost.

Jay's Laws of Leadership:

(1) Changing things is central to leadership, and changing them before anyone else is creativeness.

(2) To build something that endures, it is of great importance to have a long tenure in office—to rule for many years. Quick success can be achieved in a year or two, but nearly all great tycoons have continued their building much longer.

The Kerr-Martin Law:

In dealing with their own problems, faculty members are the world's most extreme conservatives. In dealing with other people's problems, they are the world's most extreme liberals.

Ben Franklin's Laws:

(1) Some are weatherwise, some are otherwise.

(2) There never was a good knife made of bad steel.

(3) Poverty wants some things, luxury many things, avarice all things.

(4) Keep yourself from the opportunity, and God will keep you from sin.

(5) A false friend and a shadow stay around only while the sun shines.

Velonis' Rules on Manufacturing and Specifying:

(1) After an instrument has been fully assembled and working, extra components will be found on the bench.

(2) Manufacturers' spec sheets will be incorrect by a factor of 0.5 or 2.0, depending on which multiplier gives the most optimistic value. For salesmen's claims, these factors will be 0.1 or 10.0.

Bradley's Rule:

Flattery is the sincerest form of lying.

Ward's Old Swedish Corollary:

 If cows could fly, everyone would carry an umbrella.

Arthur Schopenhauer's Theorem:

> The amount of noise which anyone can bear undisturbed stands in inverse proportion to his mental capacity.

Dr. Sloves's Theorem:

> The qualities that most attract a woman to a man are usually the same ones she can't stand years later.

Dr. Sloves's Rule:

> That which we resist the most is what we become.

David Brinkley's Observation:

> Stupidity is an almost sovereign force.

John Knowles's Law:

> Truth is plural and contingent.

Sherman's Conclusion:

> Rationalization is a mental technique which allows one to lie or cheat without feeling guilty.

Foster's Thought:

> If polls are so accurate, why are there so many polling companies?

Manfredi's Rule of Government:

> The arguments against taking action are always superior to those favoring it.

Henry Ford's Rumination:

> Under pressure, the mouth speaks when the brain is disengaged, and, sometimes unwittingly, the gearshift is in reverse when it should be in neutral.

Fishbein's Observation:
> The tire is only flat on the bottom.

Price's Principle:
> As we look ahead, time is interminable. As we look back, it is infinitesimal.

Bradford's Law:
> You can definitely make mistakes, but you can't make mistakes indefinitely.

Segal's Law:
> A man with one watch knows what time it is; a man with two watches is never sure.

The Worker's Dilemmas, or the Management's Put-Down Laws:
> (1) No matter how much you do, you'll never do enough.
> (2) What you don't do is always more important than what you do do.

Finagle's New Laws of Information:
> (1) The information we have is not what we want.
> (2) The information we want is not what we need.
> (3) The information we need is not available.

Eastman's Personnel Director's Law:
> Anyone who thinks there is some good in everyone hasn't interviewed enough people.

Stewart's Marriage Counsel Homily:
> If you can't realize your ideal, idealize the real.

Sunny Jim's Law:
> There's having and there's getting. Those who have, will always get. Those who get, will never have.

Ellenberg's Corollary:

> If a man fools me once—shame on him. If the same man fools me twice—shame on me.

Peers's Observation:

> Cheetahs are the world's fastest land animal. However, since they are never raced, cheetahs can never win.

ABOUT THE AUTHORS

John Peers, as President of LOMAC, a computer manufacturer located in Sunnyvale, California was often referred to as the Monty Python of the computer industry, and it was his own truism (PEERS'S LAW: *The solution to a problem changes the nature of the problem*) that served as inspiration for this book.

Gordon Bennett is President of Gordon Bennett & Associates, Inc., the public relations firm for the Logical Machine Corporation (LOMAC).

Cartoonist George Booth's sketches appear regularly in *The New Yorker*. He has also published two collections of his drawings: *Think Good Thoughts About a Pussycat* and *Rehearsal's Off!*